What Is Redaction Criticism?

What Is Redaction Criticism?

by
Norman Perrin

Fortress Press
Philadelphia

Second Printing 1970
Third Printing 1971
Fourth Printing 1973
Fifth Printing 1974
Sixth Printing 1976
Seventh Printing 1978

Biblical quotations from the Revised Standard Version
of the Bible, copyrighted 1946 and 1952 by the Division
of Christian Education of the National Council of
Churches, are used by permission.

Library of Congress Catalog Card No. 72-81529

ISBN 0-8006-0181-5

7068A78   Printed in the U.S.A.   1-181

Editor's Foreword

In New Testament scholarship insights, concerns, and positions may not change as much or as fast as they do in the natural sciences. But over the years they do change, and change a great deal, and they are changing with increasing rapidity. At an earlier period in the history of New Testament scholarship the synoptic Gospels (Matthew, Mark, and Luke) were thought to be relatively uncomplicated documents which had been put together without careful planning and which told a rather straightforward story. Today the synoptics are understood to be enormously intricate products containing subtle and ingenious literary patterns and highly developed theological interpretations. The three volumes in this series deal respectively with literary criticism, form criticism, and redaction criticism, and their purpose is to disclose something of the process whereby these disciplines have gained an enlarged understanding of the complex historical, literary, and theological factors which lie both behind and within the synoptic Gospels. The volumes on form and redaction criticism will deal exclusively with the synoptic Gospels, while the one on literary criticism will deal selectively with all the areas of the New Testament.

Literary criticism has traditionally concerned itself with such matters as the authorship of the various New Testament books, the possible composite nature of a given work, and the identity and extent of sources which may lie behind a certain document. More recently, however, biblical scholars have been paying attention to the criticism of fiction and poetry and to aesthetics and philosophy of language. Therefore the literary criticism of the New Testament has begun to reflect an interest in questions such as the relationship of content to form, the significance of structure or form for meaning, and the capacity of language to direct thought and to mold existence itself. The volume on literary criticism in this series will be sensitive to both the older and the newer aspects of the discipline.

The purpose of form criticism has been to get behind the sources which literary criticism might identify and to describe what was happening as the tradition about Jesus was handed on orally from person to person and from community to community. Form criticism has been especially concerned with the modifications which the life and thought of the church—both Jewish-Christian and gentile-Christian—have introduced into the tradition, and form critics have worked out criteria for distinguishing those strata in the Gospels which reflect the concerns of the church from the stratum that might be thought to go back to the historical Jesus. It has been shown that the church's vital life not only exerted a creative influence on the content of the tradition but also contributed formal characteristics, making it possible to classify much of the material in the synoptics according to literary form. Form criticism has concerned itself largely with investigating the individual units—stories and sayings—in the synoptic Gospels.

Redaction criticism is the most recent of the three disciplines to have become a self-conscious method of inquiry. It grew out of form criticism, and it presupposes and continues the procedures of the earlier discipline while extending and intensifying certain of them. The redaction critic investigates how smaller units—both simple and composite—from the oral tradition or from written sources were put together to form larger complexes, and he is especially interested in the formation of the Gospels as finished products. Redaction criticism is concerned with the interaction between an inherited tradition and a later interpretive point of view. Its goals are to understand why the items from the tradition were modified and connected as they were, to identify the theological motifs that were at work in composing a finished Gospel, and to elucidate the theological point of view which is expressed in and through the composition. Although redaction criticism has been most closely associated with the Gospels, there is no reason why it could not be used—and actually it is being used—to illuminate the relationship between tradition and interpretation in other New Testament books.

While each of the volumes in this series deals separately and focally with one of the methods of critical inquiry, each author is also aware of the other two methods. It has seemed wise to treat each of the three kinds of criticism separately for the purposes of definition, analysis, and clarification, but it should be quite clear that in actual practice the three are normally used together. They are not really separable. A New Testament scholar, in interpreting any book or shorter text or motif, would allow all three of the critical disciplines to contribute to his interpretation. An effort to demonstrate this inseparability might be made by taking a brief look at Mark 2:18–20:

> 18Now John's disciples and the Pharisees were fasting; and people came and said to him, "Why do John's disciples and the disciples of the Pharisees fast, but your disciples do not fast?" 19And Jesus said to them, "Can the wedding guests fast while the bridegroom is with them? As long as they have the bridegroom with them, they cannot fast. 20The days will come, when the bridegroom is taken away from them, and then they will fast in that day.

This passage appears not only in Mark but is also a part of that substantial portion of Mark which serves as a source for Matthew and Luke (cf. Matt. 9:14–15; Luke 5:33–35) (literary criticism). Its outstanding formal features are a brief narrative (18) that provides a setting for a saying of Jesus (19a) which takes the form of a question and which is the real interest of the passage (form criticism). The question of fasting and the use of wedding imagery suggest a Jewish point of origin. At the same time we see a break with fasting and the attribution of joyful significance to the present—*today* is a wedding—rather than waiting for the future. These features suggest a modification of the Jewish setting. On the other hand, there is nothing, at least in 18–19a, which expresses the church's faith in Jesus' resurrection or the theological interpretation of Jesus' mission which grew out of that faith. This particular relationship to Judaism, on the one hand, and to distinctly Christian theology, on the other, gives to 18–19a a good claim to reflect the situation of the historical Jesus. However, 20 (and perhaps 19b) seems to grow out of a setting later than Jesus' own. Here we see the church basing the practice of fasting on Jesus' death (form criticism).

Our text is included in a collection of stories all of which present Jesus in conflict with the Jewish authorities (2:1–3:6) and which are concluded by the statement that Jesus' enemies took counsel how they might destroy him. Mark may have found the stories already collected, and a predecessor may also have added the concluding statement. But we do not know why the predecessor might have added it, while we can imagine why Mark would have. Jesus' death was very important for him, and it assumes a prominent place in his Gospel (redaction criticism).

If we might call the form of the Gospel as a whole a comedy which overcomes tragedy—the defeat of death by resurrection—we may then grasp the significance of our brief passage in that larger pattern. The slight allusion to Jesus' death anticipates the more direct hint in 3:6, which in turn prepares for the definite predictions of Jesus' death which begin at 8:31, predictions which are fulfilled in the final chapters of the Gospel. At the same time the resurrection is anticipated by the theme of the joyousness of today, which is further deepened by the note of irrepressible newness that appears in 2:21-22 (literary criticism). Our short text contributes to Mark's presentation of the reasons for Jesus' death —he challenged the established religious order—and Mark's understanding of the significance of Jesus' death and resurrection—a new, festal day has dawned offering to man freedom from compulsive ritualism (redaction and literary criticism).

It is hoped that the three volumes in this series will give to the interested layman new insight into how biblical criticism has illuminated the nature and meaning of the New Testament.

DAN O. VIA, JR.
University of Virginia

Contents

I

The Origins of a Discipline

Redaction criticism is an attempt to represent in English the German word *Redaktionsgeschichte,* which Willi Marxsen[1] proposed as the designation for a discipline within the field of New Testament studies, a discipline that has come very much to the fore within the past two decades. It is concerned with studying the theological motivation of an author as this is revealed in the collection, arrangement, editing, and modification of traditional material, and in the composition of new material or the creation of new forms within the traditions of early Christianity. Although the discipline is called redaction criticism, it could equally be called "composition criticism"[2] because it is concerned with the composition of new material and the arrangements of redacted or freshly created material into new units and patterns, as well as with the redaction of existing material. To date redaction

[1]W. Marxsen, *Der Evangelist Markus* (Göttingen: Vandenhoeck & Ruprecht, [1]1956, [2]1959), p. 11 (English translation: *Mark the Evangelist* [New York and Nashville: Abingdon Press, 1969], p. 21). The English translation of Marxsen's book uses "redaction history" for *Redaktionsgeschichte* and "form history" for *Formgeschichte.* These literal translations ignore the convention of building on the model provided by the English term "literary criticism," a procedure that has resulted in the term "form criticism" gaining widespread acceptance and that would seem to recommend the term "redaction criticism" for the newer discipline. Marxsen's translators testify to the force of this convention when they call the practitioners of *Formgeschichte* "form critics" (p. 16)!

[2]In fact the term *Kompositionsgeschichte* (composition criticism) has been proposed for the discipline by E. Haenchen, *Der Weg Jesu* (Berlin: Alfred Töpelmann, 1966), p. 24.

criticism has been restricted to the synoptic evangelists, the authors of the Gospels of Matthew, Mark, and Luke, although there is no theoretical reason for this limitation. To the extent that we can determine the traditional material that he has used, we could do a redaction-critical study of Paul or of John, the fourth evangelist. (The first instance of a successful redaction-critical study of John is noted below on p. 85.)

The prime requisite for redaction criticism is the ability to trace the form and content of material used by the author concerned or in some way to determine the nature and extent of his activity in collecting and creating, as well as in arranging, editing, and composing. The most successful redaction-critical work has been done on the Gospels of Matthew and Luke, since in these we have one major source which each evangelist used, the Gospel of Mark, and can reconstruct a good deal of another, the sayings source "Q." But similar work can be done wherever the use of traditional material can be determined or the particular activity of the author detected, and it is interesting to note that redaction criticism really began with work on the Gospel of Mark for reasons that are noted below (see pp. 7 ff.).

In the field of New Testament criticism, the discipline of redaction criticism is the latest of the three major developments which are the subjects of the volumes in this series: literary criticism, form criticism, and redaction criticism. Though the distinctions between the three disciplines are somewhat artificial, they do call attention to the fact that the critical work has proceeded by stages and that one type of work builds upon the results of another. Form criticism and redaction criticism in particular are very closely related to one another. They are in fact the first and second stages of a unified discipline, but their divergence in emphasis is sufficient to justify their being treated separately. The present writer, however, would be the first to admit the artificiality of this procedure, especially since in a previous work he included in what he called "the form-critical approach" to the Gospels elements from both form and redaction criticism,

2

with no attempt to distinguish them from one another as they are here being distinguished.[3]

We noted earlier that the most successful redaction-critical work had been done on Matthew and Luke, but that the earliest work was done on Mark. The reason for the latter is that redaction criticism had its roots in the rejection of the so-called Marcan hypothesis. We shall now attempt to trace the background and development of this "Marcan hypothesis" at the very considerable risk of oversimplifying the issues involved.

FROM REIMARUS TO WREDE:
THE RISE AND FALL OF THE MARCAN HYPOTHESIS[4]

The story really begins with Hermann Samuel Reimarus, a professor of oriental languages in a *Gymnasium* in Hamburg, who lived from 1694 to 1768 and was very much a man of the Enlightenment. Living in a seaport which had close commercial contacts with English ports, he became aware of the work of the English Deists and was much influenced by them. Thus he came to accept a rationalistic view of religion, in which the essential truths were those of the existence of a wise and good Creator and of the immortality of the soul. These truths he held to be discernible by reason and to constitute the basis of a universal religion which could lead to happiness. Reimarus's natural, rational religion was irreconcilable with a revealed religion such as orthodox Christianity, which, because it could never be intelligible and credible to all men, could never become a universal religion. During his lifetime he wrote and published a number of works advocating his naturalistic Deism, but his major work was a defense of it against its immediate rival, orthodox Christianity: a four-thousand-page manuscript entitled *Apologie oder Schutzschrift für die vernünftigen Verehrer Gottes* (An Apol-

---

[3]N. Perrin, *Rediscovering the Teaching of Jesus* (New York: Harper & Row, 1967), pp. 15–32; hereafter cited as *Rediscovering*.

[4]For more detail on what is to follow, see A. Schweitzer's famous and brilliant *The Quest of the Historical Jesus* (New York: Macmillan, 1961 [=1910]); hereafter cited as *Quest*. A briefer survey and discussion of the issues down to the present day is given in Perrin, *Rediscovering*, pp. 207–48, 262–66 (annotated bibliography).

ogetic for the Rational Worshipers of God) which he refrained from publishing. After his death, however, G. E. Lessing (1729–81), a German Enlightenment man of letters, came across the manuscript and from the town of Wolfenbüttel published parts of it as "Wolfenbüttel Fragments by an Unnamed Author." There were seven of these fragments, and their purpose, especially that of the sixth and seventh ("Concerning the Resurrection Story" and "On the Purpose of Jesus and that of his Disciples"), was to discredit the origins of Christianity. Reimarus attempts to show that Jesus was an unsuccessful political messianic pretender, that the disciples were disappointed charlatans who invented the early Christian faith rather than go back to working for a living after the debacle of the crucifixion, and that they stole the body of Jesus in order to have an empty tomb to support their story of a resurrection! But Reimarus's work is more important than his own conscious purpose, or even than his own conclusions. Reimarus was in fact the first great Enlightenment historian to work on the Gospel narratives, and his importance lies in the effect that his work has had on our understanding of the nature of those narratives. Reimarus has shown that, if we accept the Enlightenment view that history is "what actually happened," then the Gospels are not historical, since many of their narratives reflect concepts that were developed long after the events they purport to narrate took place. Reimarus shows the necessity of assuming a "creative element in the tradition" to which are to be ascribed "the miracles, the stories which turn on the fulfilment of messianic prophecy, the universalistic traits and the predictions of the passion and the resurrection."[5] So far as redaction criticism is concerned, it is this "creative element in the tradition," as Albert Schweitzer calls it, which concerns us, and in calling attention to it Reimarus is the father of our discipline, as he is of Life of Jesus research altogether.

The mantle of Reimarus descended upon David Friedrich Strauss (1808–74) whose *Das Leben Jesu, kritisch bearbeitet* (English translation: *The Life of Jesus, Critically Examined*

[5]Schweitzer, *Quest*, p. 24.

4

[1846]) published in two volumes in 1835 and 1836 really sets the stage for "the Marcan hypothesis." The effect of Strauss's work—as of Reimarus's—is to call attention to "a creative element" in the Gospel narratives. For him, these narratives are to a large extent expressions of "myth," i.e., they express religious concepts derived from Judaism or Hellenism, from the Old Testament or Christian experience. In their present form they cannot be understood as historical, nor can a residue from them be rescued as historical by explaining away the element of the miraculous in them. The Gospel narratives are essentially concerned with purveying a Christ myth and this fact has to be recognized about them.

Reimarus had refrained from publishing his work, but not so Strauss! He wrote for immediate publication and upon publication he became the center of a storm of controversy, remarkable both for its bitterness and its barrenness. "Scarcely ever has a book let loose such a storm of controversy; and scarcely ever has a controversy been so barren of immediate result."[6] So far as the rise of redaction criticism is concerned, however, the impact of Strauss's work was far from barren—even though the results were not immediate. The long-term effect of his work was to call attention to the role of religious conceptions or "myth," in the formation of Gospel materials. In the twentieth century Rudolf Bultmann, who was consciously indebted to Strauss, would utilize Strauss's insights to make his own contribution to the development of redaction criticism.

A more immediate result of Strauss's work was the promulgation of the "Marcan hypothesis." In effect what happened was that Strauss's efforts made an impact on New Testament scholars of a liberal theological persuasion—an impact which was very strong but which left them feeling pulled in two different ways at the same time. On the one hand, they had to accept the force of a good deal of his argumentation: The Gospel narratives *were* to a large extent the products of myth. On the other hand, however, they were unprepared to abandon the idea of knowing Jesus "as he actually was" and settle

Ibid., p. 96.

for a Christ myth. In their dilemma they seized upon a newly developed literary-critical insight, namely, the view that Mark was the earliest Gospel and a source used by Matthew and Luke. This idea, developed through successive works by C. Lachmann (1835), C. G. Wilke, and H. Weisse (both 1838), reached its climax in 1863 with H. J. Holtzmann's epoch-making *Die Synoptischen Evangelien. Ihr Ursprung und geschichtlicher Charakter* (The Synoptic Gospels. Their Origin and Historical Character).[7] From this point on it came to be an accepted canon of Life of Jesus research that Mark was the earliest of the Gospels, that it was the closest in point of time to the original eyewitnesses, and that it could be used with confidence as a historical source for knowledge of the ministry of Jesus. However much we may have to recognize that Matthew and Luke, as later productions of the church, have been influenced by theological conceptions, etc., Mark, the earliest and nearest to the events themselves, remains comparatively free from such theological conceptions and is a reliable source for historical knowledge of Jesus. Although not himself a direct representative of the German tradition, B. F. Westcott penned words in 1851 which characterize the spirit of that age of scholarship: "The Gospel of St. Mark, conspicuous for its vivid simplicity, seems to be the most direct representative of the first evangelic tradition, the common foundation on which the others were reared." Further:

In substance and style and treatment the Gospel of St. Mark is essentially a transcript from life. The course and the issue of facts are imaged in it in the clearest outline. If all other arguments against the mythic origin of the Evangelic narratives were wanting, this vivid and simple record, stamped with the most distinct impress of independence and originality . . . would be sufficient to refute a theory subversive of all faith in history.[8]

---

[7]On these works see Schweitzer, *Quest,* pp. 121–36, 203–5, and any standard history of the synoptic problem, e.g., P. Feine, J. Behm, W. G. Kümmel, *Introduction to the New Testament,* trans. A. J. Mattil, Jr. (New York and Nashville: Abingdon Press, 1966), pp. 37–42.

[8]B. F. Westcott, *Introduction to the Study of the Gospels* (New York: Macmillan, 1882 [= 1851]), pp. 213, 369.

In this reaction to Strauss we find, first, that Mark is being accepted as the earliest Gospel on sound literary-critical grounds, and, secondly, that, as the earliest Gospel, it is accepted as a reliable historical source. This second point, however, is not based upon any argument from recognizable academic criteria but upon the simple assumption that, as the earliest and nearest to the events, it must be historical, an assumption supported by references to the realistic character of the narratives or the like. This is the Marcan hypothesis: that Mark is both the earliest Gospel, a source used by Matthew and Luke, and a reliable historical source; as such it provides the basis for a Life of Jesus. The earlier reliance upon Matthew and John as the work of the apostles whose names they bear was replaced, under the impact of the work of Strauss, with a reliance upon Mark, the earliest of the Gospels and the one with the historical order and the realistic narratives.

The first stirrings of what came to be redaction criticism are to be observed in the context of a discussion of precisely this understanding of Mark. The starting point for redaction criticism is a debate about the Marcan hypothesis. It is not about the fact that it is the earliest of the Gospels—that has remained the opinion of mainstream critical scholarship from Holtzmann to the present—but about the assumption that, as the earliest, it is a reliable historical source. In particular it is a debate about the contention that this "vivid and simple record" is the major argument against "the mythic view of the Evangelic narratives." This brings us to Wilhelm Wrede (1859–1906), who sounded the death knell for this kind of view by demonstrating that a major aspect of the Marcan narratives was precisely the "mythic" and, in so doing, opened the door for the entry of redaction criticism upon the scene.

Wrede's contribution to our discussion is his book *Das Messiasgeheimnis in den Evangelien* (The Messianic Secret in the Gospels), which was published in 1901[9] and is not so much

[9] Göttingen: Vandenhoeck & Ruprecht. Unchanged second and third editions were published in 1913 and 1963. An English translation has recently been announced but not yet published.

a contribution to a discussion as a bombshell! Few books have had such a drastic and far-reaching consequence in a given field of study as this one; so far as Gospel studies and Life of Jesus research were concerned, nothing would ever be the same again. Wrede showed once and for all that it was impossible to read Mark as a vivid, simple record unless one read as much *into* Mark as he read *from* it, and he showed that the narratives in Mark are permeated through and through with a theological conception—that of the Messianic Secret—which necessarily was of post-Easter origin. In other words, those whom we shall call the "historicizers," those who read Mark as fundamentally a historical record, were bringing their history to Mark rather than taking it from him, and they were also closing their eyes to a major feature of the actual Marcan narratives.

The arguments of Wrede's book are necessarily detailed, involving as they do careful observation and exegesis of the whole Gospel of Mark and comparison of text with text throughout the Gospel. For this reason it is impossible to summarize his arguments; their true force is cumulative and can only be grasped by reading them in their entirety. But a sample of the way he argues must be given in order to illustrate the newness and force of what he was doing. We shall take as our example his discussion of the way in which throughout the Gospel the disciples are portrayed as misunderstanding aspects of Jesus and his ministry. This is a theme which runs throughout Mark's Gospel; for example: in verse 4:13 the disciples do not understand the parable of the sower; in verses 4:30 f. they do not understand Jesus' power over the elements; in 6:50–52 they understand neither the first feeding of the multitude nor the walking on the water; in 7:18 they do not understand the distinction between clean and unclean; in 8:16–21 they understand neither the "leaven of the Pharisees" nor either of the feedings; in 9:5 f. they understand neither the nature nor the meaning of the transfiguration; in 10:24–26 they do not understand the difficulty riches create for entering the kingdom; in 14:37–41 they are completely confused at Gethsemane. Thus, the disciples' misunderstanding is a consistent theme running through the story, from Galilee to Gethsemane, and is related to the words and deeds of Jesus as well as to the events which the disciples are privileged to witness. Moreover, the same misunderstanding is to be found in connection with the predictions of the passion; each of these is met by this inability to understand: in verse 8:31 f. it is Peter who misunderstands; in 9:30–32 it is all disciples; in 10:32–34 the disciples' misunderstanding is described in terms of their being "amazed"; and in 10:35–40 James and John display their misunderstanding by the request they make. Nor is it simply the prospect of the humiliation of the passion which the disciples cannot grasp, for neither can they grasp the prospective glory of the resurrection (9:10).

The fact that these references are to be found throughout the Gospel and in connection with so many different aspects of Jesus and his ministry gives rise to the supposition that they represent the evangelist's conception rather than historical actuality. This supposition can be supported by observing that they often occur in contexts which clearly reflect the actual literary details of preceding narratives and which are therefore probably additions, e.g., 6:50–52 and 8:16–21. Further, a historicizing approach to the narratives, which attempts to explain them as representing historical actuality, has to read into the texts things that are not there. For example, it could be argued that the disciples only gradually came to understand Jesus as the Messiah, and that when they did they had a false understanding of messiahship. But where is there any support for this in the texts themselves? There is no progression of understanding here; the disciples are as imperceptive about Jesus at the end as they were at the beginning; in this regard they neither change, develop, nor progress. Nor is there any evidence that their failure to understand is limited to, or even especially linked with, the idea of humiliation and suffering in connection with the Messiah; they understand neither suffering nor glory. Finally, that they were influenced by a false idea of messiahship is a hypothesis for which there is not one word of evidence in the text of Mark.[10]

Using such arguments Wrede deals with varied aspects of the Marcan narratives. He shows that only by ignoring what the narratives actually say and by reading into them one's own ideas is it possible to regard these narratives as historical. This is the first aspect of Wrede's work; he cuts the ground from under the feet of the Marcan hypothesis by demonstrating that major aspects of the Marcan narratives are not in fact historical. But if they are not historical, they must represent a dogmatic idea held by the author or an idea which is at work in the tradition. This brings us to the second aspect of Wrede's work, i.e., his claim that a major theme in the narratives of Mark, that of the Messianic Secret, represents in fact a dogmatic idea at work in the tradition.

Throughout the Marcan narratives there is an emphasis upon the necessity to keep secret Jesus' messiahship. Jesus commands the demons not to make him known (1:25; 1:34; 3:12); he demands the same silence regarding his other miracles (1:43–45; 5:35–43, esp. vss. 37, 40, and 43; 7:31–37, esp. vss. 33 and 36; 8:22–26, esp. vss. 23 and 26); he commands silence after Peter's confession (8:30) and after the transfiguration (9:9). Nor is this theme limited to specific commands of Jesus. He is represented as attempting in general to remain incognito (7:24; 9:30 f.); and in the account of the blind man at Jericho even the bystanders (or disciples) issue a command to be silent (10:48). In all of these instances the commands are presented in an abrupt and stereotyped manner, and no motive for them is ever given. All attempts to explain this demand for silence as a historical aspect of the ministry of Jesus break down, as Wrede shows convincingly, and therefore we must recognize that this Messianic Secret has no historical basis in the life of Jesus; it is a theological conception at work in the tradition.[11] The clue to understanding this conception is to be found in 9:9: "And as they were coming down the mountain, he charged them

---

[10]We have reproduced in our own words the main threads of the argument in Wrede, *Messiasgeheimnis*, pp. 82–110.

[11]Wrede, *Messiasgeheimnis*, p. 66.

to tell no one what they had seen, until the Son of man should have risen from the dead." The messiahship of Jesus is and must be a secret during his lifetime on earth, but with the resurrection the secret is revealed. The theological conception of the Messianic Secret is rooted in the fact that Jesus was not recognized as Messiah by the disciples, nor by anyone, before the resurrection. After the resurrection he *is* so recognized. However, the messiahship ascribed to him reflects the concept as it was understood in early Christianity, a concept which combines elements from a Jewish conception of "messiah" (such as would fit a man like Simon bar Cochba, the messianic pretender who led a revolt against Rome in 133 A.D.) and elements from the idea—quite foreign to Judaism— of a supernatural Son of God. In this combination the supernatural Son of God elements are dominant, and, in Mark, Jesus is always presented in this manner. In word and in deed he always acts with supernatural authority, and he is always seen as having this authority whatever title is ascribed to him. Even in the sayings where he is presented as the Son of man who must suffer, he is still thought of as supernatural Son of God, which is why later generations found the sayings hard to understand: "The predictions of the passion appear mysterious and incomprehensible not from the standpoint of the actual circumstances of the life of Jesus, but from the dramatic perspective of a later time which found the paradox of the divine counsel in the suffering and death of Jesus."[12] But a presentation of Jesus as the Messiah-Son of God of early Christianity must stand in tension with actual traditions about his life and death. These actual traditions cannot contain anything of the Christian messianic idea—an idea which was developed later in a situation that the earlier traditions did not envisage. It is this tension that the literary device of the Messianic Secret is designed to overcome. The narratives present Jesus as keeping his messiahship secret during his earthly life and claim that it was to be revealed only after the resurrection. The latter aspect reflects the historical actuality; the former is the device by means of which it is shown to have been possible for Jesus to have

[12]*Ibid.*, p. 110.

acted as (Christian) Messiah-Son of God during his lifetime and yet to have been acknowledged as such, even by
his disciples, only after his death and resurrection. Moreover,
the fact that this Messianic Secret is a literary device read
into the narratives as they were developing in the tradition
is evidenced by their inconsistency regarding the secret. In
the narratives themselves Jesus commands secrecy yet often
publicly acts as Messiah-Son of God; he enjoins silence in
some instances but not in others, and so on.

This then is Wrede's presentation of the Messianic Secret
in Mark, a truly epoch-making event in the history of the
study of the Gospels. Today we recognize that there are
many things about his thesis that we would want to modify—
after all, more than sixty years of work on these texts is bound
to have made many changes necessary in any thesis—but still
we recognize as justifiable the two fundamental claims Wrede
made. These claims have been fully confirmed by subsequent
research: Mark may be read in a historicizing manner only
by reading all kinds of things into the text, and that text
itself is what it is largely because of dogmatic ideas that were
at work in the tradition. "In this sense," says Wrede himself
with complete justification, "the gospel of Mark belongs to
the history of Christian dogma."[13]

So far as the development of redaction criticism is concerned, Wrede's thesis opened the way for the study of the
dogmatic ideas and theological conceptions that were at
work in the tradition. The study of these ideas and conceptions is the task of redaction criticism, and Wrede's work on
the Messianic Secret is in many ways the first product of this
discipline. But here we would have to admit the importance
of those sixty years which separate his work from ours, for
there are two things that had to happen before redaction
criticism could really flower. First, we had to learn to think
of the evangelists and their predecessors who were at work
in the tradition in a more positive manner than Wrede was
prepared to do. Having a comparatively low opinion of the
abilities of the evangelist Mark and being inclined to mini-
mize Mark's impact upon the tradition, Wrede emphasized

[13]*Ibid.*, p. 131.

that the dogmatic ideas were developed through a rather impersonal historical process. Redaction criticism, on the other hand, tends to think of the evangelist as having a much more positive and creative role than this. Secondly, in order for redaction criticism proper to develop we had to learn to trace the various stages through which tradition has passed. Only then was it possible to recognize the nature and extent of the redaction. In other words redaction criticism proper is dependent upon the ability to write a history of the tradition. This Wrede did not have the tools to do, since these tools were developed through the later discipline known as form criticism.

FORM CRITICISM

As we stated earlier in this chapter, form and redaction criticism belong together and may indeed be regarded as the first and second stages of one common enterprise. Nonetheless, their emphases are distinct from one another and to view form criticism simply as the preparation for redaction criticism is wholly unjust and unjustifiable. But that is what we must do here, and we plead as an excuse—not as a justification—the necessary limits to this present volume and the fact that another volume in this series is devoted to form criticism itself. This is also our excuse for ignoring, in what follows, the fact that form criticism of the New Testament texts was developed only after form criticism had already been applied to secular literature and to the Old Testament.

Just as redaction criticism first appears in the work of Wilhelm Wrede, so much of what later came to be known as form criticism is intimated in the work of Julius Wellhausen (1844–1918). After almost a lifetime of work in the fields of Old Testament and Semitic languages, in which fields he was a tremendously important pioneer, Wellhausen turned to New Testament studies and published commentaries on Matthew, Mark, and Luke, and an "Introduction to the First Three Gospels."[14] In these works many of what came to be the

---

[14]J. Wellhausen, *Das Evangelium Matthaei* (Berlin: Georg Reimer, 1904); *Das Evangelium Marci* (Berlin: Georg Reimer, 1903); *Das Evangelium Lucae* (Berlin: Georg Reimer, 1904); *Einleitung in die drei ersten Evangelien* (Berlin: Georg Reimer, 1905).

characteristic emphases of twentieth century synoptic scholarship first found expression. The books are amazingly prophetic of what was to come, although only a careful reading of them will disclose this. Wellhausen is "inclined to throw out far-reaching hints rather than to establish definite conclusions";[15] he presents his material discursively rather than systematically. But in his discussion of Mark he makes three points that were to be developed into major axioms by the form critics. These are: (1) the original source for the material in the Gospel is oral tradition in which that material circulated in small units; (2) this material has been brought together and redacted in various ways and at various stages, only one of which is that of the evangelist; and (3) such material gives us information about the beliefs and circumstances of the early church as well as about the ministry of Jesus.[16] These themes, stated by Wellhausen in the period immediately before the First World War, were seeds which came to full fruition in the work of the form critics immediately after that war. The war itself necessarily called a halt to academic biblical study in Germany. When it was resumed there was a "new look" to that study. Independently of one another, three scholars produced works which shared the common emphases and concerns of form criticism. These scholars were Karl Ludwig Schmidt (1891–1956), Martin Dibelius (1883–1947), and Rudolf Bultmann (1884–).[17]

[15]R. H. Lightfoot, *History and Interpretation in the Gospels* (New York: Harper and Bros., no date), p. 22; hereafter cited as *History and Interpretation.*

[16]Wellhausen, *Einleitung*, pp. 43–57; *Marci*, passim. See also the statement by Lightfoot, *History and Interpretation*, p. 23.

[17]K. L. Schmidt, *Der Rahmen der Geschichte Jesu* (Berlin: Trowitzsch & Sohn, 1919), hereafter cited as *Rahmen;* M. Dibelius, *Die Formgeschichte des Evangeliums* (Tübingen: J. C. B. Mohr [Paul Siebeck], 1919); R. Bultmann, *Die Geschichte der synoptischen Tradition* (Göttingen: Vandenhoeck & Ruprecht, 1921). Schmidt's book was not subsequently revised, nor has it been translated into English. Dibelius's book went through several revised editions of which the most recent is ⁴1961, and it was translated into English by B. L. Woolf as *From Tradition to Gospel* (New York: Charles Scribner's Sons, 1935); hereafter cited as *Tradition.* Bultmann's book was also revised several times, the most recent edition being ⁵1961, and it was translated (very badly) by J. Marsh as *The History of the Synoptic Tradition* (New York: Harper & Row, 1963); hereafter cited as *History.*

14

Schmidt concerned himself with the framework of the Gospel narratives, showing that this framework was normally supplied by the evangelist himself, who had taken small units of tradition and fitted them loosely together in accordance with his own interests and concerns. He reached the conclusion: "On the whole there is [in the Gospels] no life of Jesus in the sense of a developing story, as a chronological outline of the history of Jesus, but only isolated stories, pericopes, which have been provided with a framework."[18] Dibelius started with that activity in the early church in which the tradition now found in the Gospels was first used ("In the beginning was the sermon")[19] and studied the forms the tradition would have had in that setting, analyzing them and tracing their history down to that of the Gospel form itself. Bultmann took as his point of departure the Gospels themselves and worked back from the material as it is found there to the earlier forms of it that can be traced in the prior tradition. So Dibelius and Bultmann have essentially the same concern and cover essentially the same ground, but they start at opposite ends and move, therefore, in opposite directions, Dibelius forward to the Gospels and Bultmann backward from them.

Rather than give more details of the work of the individual form critics, we shall summarize their common ideas and emphases:

(1) The Gospels as we now have them are not single creations out of a whole cloth but consist of collections of material, the final selection and arrangement of which we owe to the evangelists themselves. Mark is here the primary influence; he created the literary form "Gospel" and Matthew and Luke both follow him and use his material.

[18]Schmidt, *Rahmen*, p. 317. This is the closing sentence of the book.
[19]This famous and oft quoted dictum of Dibelius is not actually in *From Tradition to Gospel* where we find only: "In the sermon the elements of the future Christian literature lay side by side as in a mother cell" (p. 70). It is from "Die alttestamentlichen Motive in der Leidensgeschichte des Petrus-und des Johannes-Evangeliums," *Zeitschrift für die alttestamentliche Wissenschaft. Beiheft*, 33 (Giessen: Alfred Töpelmann, 1918), 125, and it actually reads: "At the beginning of all early Christian creativity there stands the sermon: missionary and hortatory preaching, narrative and parenesis, prophecy and the interpretation of scripture."

(2) The material now presented in the Gospels has a previous history of use in the church, largely a history of oral transmission. It circulated in the church in the form of individual units or small collections of related material and in this form it served definite functions in the life and worship of the church, in preaching and apologetic, in exhortation and instruction.

(3) The smallest units of tradition, the individual story, saying, dialogue, etc., have definite forms which can be defined and studied. Each of these forms served a definite function in a concrete situation in the life of the early church. This situation is what is referred to as the *Sitz im Leben* of the material.

The main purpose for the creation, the circulation, and the use of these forms was not to preserve the history of Jesus, but to strengthen the life of the church. Thus these forms reflect the concern of the church, and both the form and content have been influenced by the faith and theology of the church, as well as by her situation and practice.

The form critics who concern us most are Dibelius and Bultmann, and despite their broad measure of agreement, there are differences of emphasis between them that are significant for the development of redaction criticism. The difference of emphasis which concerns us is the different understanding each has of what is historical (i.e., relating to the historical Jesus) in the tradition and, parallel to this, the different estimate of the extent to which the faith and theology of the early church affected the formation and modification of that tradition.

Let us begin with Dibelius. He can say roundly:

> The first understanding afforded by the standpoint of Form-geschichte is that there never was a "purely" historical witness to Jesus. Whatever was told of Jesus' words and deeds was always a testimony of faith as formulated for preaching and exhortation in order to convert unbelievers and confirm the faithful. What founded Christianity was not knowledge about a historical process, but the confidence that the content of the story was salvation: the decisive beginning of the End. [Further, form criticism] . . . undertakes to portray that understanding of the story of Jesus, by which the various formulations of the material are dominated.[20]

[20]Both quotes from Dibelius, *Tradition*, p. 295.

16

At the same time Dibelius undoubtedly believes that the traditional material itself contained a solid core of historical information about Jesus, and that form criticism is an invaluable tool for the work of recovering this core. This is particularly the case with sayings and teaching material. "That the words of Jesus were preserved, that they were put together to form 'speeches' with a single theme, and . . . edited in the interest of exhortation, shows the church's concern for shaping life according to the commands of the Master."[21] In this typical Dibelius statement we can see not only the acknowledgment of the church's role in shaping the tradition (". . . put together . . . edited"), but also his conviction that "words of Jesus were preserved," that it really was "the commands of the Master" which lay at the heart of the church's endeavor. In reading Dibelius one gets the impression that he thought essentially, even if unconsciously, in terms of two major categories: the category of legendary material of various kinds created in the tradition about Jesus, as it was in the traditions about other major figures of the ancient world; and the category of material having an essentially historical basis, which was modified as it was transmitted in the tradition. With this kind of emphasis, form criticism becomes an invaluable tool for Life of Jesus research, and it was acknowledged as such by many scholars. "Thus, form criticism may be looked upon as a necessary step in research; if successful, it may lead us back to the fountain-head of Christian origins."[22] So wrote F. C. Grant in an introduction to a book whose major content is an essay by Bultmann. This statement, however, represents a decidedly Anglo-Saxon interpretation of the emphasis of Dibelius.

While it is true that Bultmann's work can also be used as a tool in Life of Jesus research—the present writer's *Rediscovering the Teaching of Jesus* uses it in this way and, in fact, owes much more to Bultmann than to Dibelius—nevertheless, Bultmann's emphasis is in some respects very different from that of Dibelius. In general Bultmann ascribes a greater element of

---

[21]Dibelius, *Tradition,* p. 289.
[22]F. C. Grant, Preface to R. Bultmann and K. Kundsin, *Form Criticism. Two Essays on New Testament Research,* trans. F. C. Grant (New York: Harper Torchbooks, 1962 [= 1934]), pp. vii.

free creativity to the early church in her work on the tradition than does Dibelius. Bultmann is neither as interested in, nor as confident of, the existence of the historical core in the teaching material as Dibelius is, and his *History of the Synoptic Tradition* gives a more negative impression of the historical element in the tradition of the teaching of Jesus than does Dibelius's *From Tradition to Gospel*. But it should be pointed out that this difference is one of emphasis rather than of essence; and it must certainly be stressed that it is Bultmann who actually analyzes the synoptic texts in great detail and Dibelius who tends to talk in more general terms! With regard to their impact upon the English-speaking world of biblical scholarship, it should also be noted that it was Dibelius who made the major impact in the nineteen thirties and forties, but that Bultmann is the more important figure today. This is because the more "positive" emphasis of Dibelius was more congenial to the Anglo-Saxon scholarship of the earlier period; however, it is Bultmann's meticulous analysis of the tradition text by text that has better stood the test of time. (Incidentally, the reader should be warned that Bultmann's book has been so badly translated that the English version gives no true impression of the force and care of the argumentation of the German original.)

The difference in emphasis between Bultmann and Dibelius, however, is not only that the former ascribes a greater element of free creativity to the early church in her work on the tradition, but also that he is much more interested than is Dibelius in the actual details of that work. He is concerned with writing a history of the synoptic tradition and, in the course of doing this, he is forced to attempt to describe and to understand the details of the processes at work in the creation and transmission of that tradition in a way that Dibelius, who is more concerned with a description of the original forms and their functions in the community's life, is not. Again the difference is one of emphasis rather than essence and it should certainly not be overstressed; but it is nonetheless there and it is the reason why redaction criticism has developed more directly from the work of Bultmann than from that of Dibelius.

In this last connection we must consider briefly the views of Dibelius and Bultmann regarding the theological motivation to be discerned in the work of the synoptic evangelists themselves. This has been the point of departure for redaction criticism as a separable aspect of the general discipline of form criticism, and we have already noted the interest of Wrede in Mark from this perspective. The views of Dibelius and Bultmann are interesting and even a brief consideration of them should correct any false impression of the extent of the differences between them, which our remarks may have created.

A difference in emphasis is here again apparent. Dibelius says that the synoptic evangelists "are not 'authors' in the literary sense, but collectors"[23] and the chapter of his book dealing with the composition of the Gospel of Mark is simply headed "Collection" [Sammlung]. Although he can speak of "the composer [der Verfasser] of the Gospel of St. Mark," his emphasis is upon "this collection of tradition."[24] Bultmann, on the other hand, has as his heading, "The Editing [Redaktion] of the Narrative Material and the Composition [Komposition] of the Gospels"[25] and speaks of "the theological character of the Gospels."[26] But the difference is more apparent than real because we also read that "Mark is not sufficiently master of his material to venture on a systematic construction himself,"[27] and, when it comes to a discussion of the "dogmatic motives" which have influenced Mark in his work of composition,[28] Bultmann is for the most part content to echo Dibelius's characterization of Mark as "the book of secret epiphanies." What is new in Bultmann is his emphasis that the purpose of

---

[23]Dibelius, Tradition, p. 59.
[24]Ibid., pp. 218, 219. The translation uses "synthesis" to translate Sammlung, but "collection" is better.
[25]Bultmann, History, p. 337. One grows weary of noting mistakes in the English version of this book. The plural "Compositions" here is one of the more obvious ones.
[26]Ibid., p. 338.
[27]Ibid., p. 350.
[28]Ibid., pp. 345 ff.

the author is "the union of the Hellenistic kerygma about Christ . . . with the tradition of the story about Jesus."[29] This goes very considerably beyond Dibelius, although it would not necessarily be foreign to him.

Bultmann also goes beyond Dibelius in concerning himself with *Redaktion* and *Komposition* in the Gospels of Matthew and Luke.[30] Here he concerns himself with the relationship to, and the differences from, the Gospel of Mark and with the theological motivation for these differences. In this he is the true father of redaction criticism, although it should be noted that he reaches conclusions very different from those reached by the redaction critics. So far as Matthew is concerned he can say: "Nevertheless, Mathew's portrayal is not so consciously motivated by dogmatic motives as was Mark's. It is much more that the Christian church's outlook is an unconscious influence in Matthew, and that is why the literary form of his work is not so dependent upon his own outlook as was the case with Mark."[31] As for Luke, "he does not permit his dogmatic conceptions to exercise any essential influence on his work," and major theological tendencies at work in his Gospel "are less characteristic of himself than of his circle and his age."[32] A Günther Bornkamm or a Hans Conzelmann would also say that the theology of Matthew or Luke, in many respects, is that of their church and their age, but they would assess very differently the influence of the theology of Matthew and Luke upon the narrative of their Gospels. We must recognize that Bultmann, although moving in the direction that led to redaction criticism, had spent so much time and effort working in the synoptic tradition itself that he could not suddenly see clearly the special uses which Matthew and Luke made of that tradition. The redaction critics, on the other hand, came a generation later and were able to build upon Bultmann's work on the tradition. Therefore they were able to

[29]*Ibid.*, p. 347.
[30]*Ibid.*, pp. 350–58 and 358–67.
[31]This is our retranslation of the German represented by the first two sentences on p. 357 of the English translation of Bultmann's *History.* That translation is simply wrong.
[32]Bultmann, *History*, p. 366.

move more readily to a special consideration of Matthew and Luke. Mark was a special case, partly because the spadework Wrede had done on Mark was something the form critics could assume, and partly because the tremendous act of creating the literary form "Gospel" as well as the theological significance of this form was always clear to them. This latter point is another reason why redaction criticism first appears in connection with the Gospel of Mark. Wrede had seen already that there were theological motives at work in Mark and that this Gospel was not—as the "Marcan hypothesis" maintained—a comparatively reliable historical source. Then too, when the significance of the fact that it was Mark who created the "Gospel" form became apparent, questions of theological motivation inevitably were raised, especially by those scholars whose work on the tradition made it possible for them to appreciate fully the uniqueness of what Mark had done.

AN ANTICIPATION OF REDACTION CRITICISM: R. H. LIGHTFOOT

Thus far we have been considering the form critics as the immediate antecedents of redaction criticism. Form criticism arose in a series of independent works which were produced after the First World War in Germany, works which turned out to be related in emphasis, as we have seen. Redaction criticism appears in a remarkably similar way after the Second World War in Germany, again in a series of independent works which turn out to be related in emphasis. But before we turn to the German scene immediately after 1946, we must consider one further work, namely, the Bampton Lectures for 1934 given by R. H. Lightfoot (1883–1953) and published as *History and Interpretation in the Gospels,* an altogether remarkable work.

English language reaction to form criticism tended to be of three types: (1) rejection of the method, either as a whole or in part; (2) acceptance of the method as a valuable tool in Life of Jesus research, an instance of which we saw above; and (3) R. H. Lightfoot! Lightfoot stands all by himself as a pioneering scholar who understood what form criticism had to offer and took it and used it; in so doing he actually reached

a new frontier beyond that reached by Dibelius and Bultmann. Although he does not use the term, Lightfoot was
actually the first redaction critic; in the ways in which he goes
beyond Dibelius and Bultmann he anticipates the methodology
that was to come into full flower in the work of Günther Bornkamm, Hans Conzelmann, and Willi Marxsen. The reason for
this is consistent with what we observed above in connection
with Bultmann, namely, that redaction criticism could only
develop from form criticism in the work of someone who could
presuppose the form-critical work done on the synoptic tradition. Bornkamm, Conzelmann, Marxsen—all these grew up as
students under the influence of Dibelius and Bultmann; they
came a generation later and so this is entirely natural. But in
the early nineteen thirties Lightfoot deliberately went to Germany to study form criticism as a possible solution to problems he had come up against in the study of the Gospels.[33]
There he encountered form criticism at first hand, was con-
verted to its approach, and was thereafter able to assume its
results in his own work. So, by the accident of personal circumstances, he was in the position that German students reached
only after 1946, for the German students of Dibelius and
Bultmann in the nineteen thirties were to have the natural
development of their work interrupted by the Third Reich and
the Second World War in a way which Lightfoot was not.
Lightfoot, however, would have anticipated them somewhat
in any event, since he came to the study in his maturity and
was therefore able to produce his own work more quickly.

Apart from the outward circumstances, that which makes
Lightfoot's work what it is, is the fact that he was able to free
himself from the major concern of his contemporaries in Gospel studies in Britain and America: Life of Jesus research.
Thus he was able to see form criticism in its own light, and to
see—better than those who saw it in relation to Life of Jesus
research—the direction in which it was to develop. Actually,
even Lightfoot testifies to the tremendous hold that Life of

[33]On this see the memoir by D. E. Nineham in *Studies in the Gospels.
Essays in Memory of R. H. Lightfoot*, ed. D. E. Nineham (Oxford: Basil
Blackwell, 1955), pp. vi–xvi.

Jesus research had upon Gospel studies in his day, because he feels compelled to say something about his own work in relation to it. So he adds a final paragraph that includes the memorable sentence: "For all the inestimable value of the gospels they yield us little more than a whisper of his (Jesus') voice; we trace in them but the outskirts of his ways." This statement aroused a storm of controversy, in the heat of which much of the true significance of Lightfoot's work tended to get lost. He must often have wished he had never penned that paragraph and certainly his work was complete without it.

In the first two Bampton Lectures Lightfoot reviews critical work on the synoptic Gospels, with special reference to Wrede and Wellhausen, and, relying mainly upon Dibelius, presents the main tenets of *Formgeschichte* (Lightfoot does not use "form criticism" but retains the German term) as they would apply to the Gospel of Mark. It is the third lecture that is most interesting in our particular context because here Lightfoot attempts "to examine the doctrine set forth in this gospel (Mark)" in light of the discipline of form criticism and finds "interpretation continually present in a book most of us were taught to regard as almost exclusively historical."[34] To all intents and purposes, this lecture is an exercise in redaction criticism. For example, Lightfoot argues that the introduction to the Gospel (1:1–13) reveals the evangelist's theological purposes and that the presentation of John the Baptist—designed as it is by the evangelist to explain who Jesus is—has a christological purpose. This latter point was to be a major emphasis in the work of Marxsen twenty years later!

But the fourth lecture also exhibits the kind of concerns that are prevalent today because in it Lightfoot explains "the content and structure of the gospel of St. Mark"; however, he does this "in the light of its main purpose," which purpose is clearly to be recognized as theological: "We have found reason to believe that, rightly regarded it [Mark's Gospel] may be called the book of the (secret) Messiahship of Jesus."[35] Over and over again narrative features of the Gospel, or aspects of the

[34]Lightfoot, *History and Interpretation*, p. 57.
[35]*Ibid.*, p. 98.

arrangement of the material, or evident selection of transitional material is explained in terms of the evangelist's theological purpose just as they would be by a redaction critic today. All in all, *History and Interpretation in the Gospels* can be read with as much profit today as it could have been at the time of its first publication; indeed, it can be read with more profit now because the discussion has at last caught up with Lightfoot, and is concerned with the same problems and issues that concerned him twenty years ago, and is using the same methodology to approach them!

II

The Flowering of
the Discipline

Redaction criticism burst into full flower immediately
after the Second World War in Germany. Just as three scholars
emerged with independent works marking the beginning of
form criticism proper after the hiatus caused by the First
World War, so three scholars came forward with independent
works denoting the beginning of redaction criticism proper
after the hiatus caused by the Second World War. After the
First World War it was Karl Ludwig Schmidt, Martin Dibelius,
and Rudolf Bultmann, as we have already noted; after the
Second World War it was Günther Bornkamm, Hans Conzelmann, and Willi Marxsen. Though working independently of
one another—Bornkamm on Matthew, Conzelmann on Luke,
and Marxsen on Mark—they moved in the same general direction. One of them, Willi Marxsen, gave the new movement its
German name, *Redaktionsgeschichte*. We shall now consider
them separately beginning with Günther Bornkamm, whose
redaction-critical work appeared first.

GÜNTHER BORNKAMM AND THE GOSPEL OF MATTHEW

Günther Bornkamm is a pupil of Bultmann and a leading
member of the so-called Bultmann school. He is therefore one
who has always assumed the results of form criticism in his
own studies. Consequently he has been able to take the discipline a stage further, and it is in his work that we first come to
redaction criticism proper. His first study on this theme was a
short article, published in the journal of the theological school

in Bethel in 1948 and now available in English in the volume *Tradition and Interpretation in Matthew*, by Bornkamm and two of his pupils, G. Barth and H. J. Held. In this study he investigates the pericope of the Stilling of the Storm in Matthew 8:23–27. By comparing it with its source, Mark 4:35–41, he shows that Matthew actually reinterprets the story as he inherits it from Mark. Thus Matthew inserts it into a definite context of its own and presents it in such a way as to give it a new meaning, a meaning which it does not have for the other evangelists: "Matthew is not only a hander-on of the narrative, but also its oldest exegete, and in fact the first to interpret the journey of the disciples with Jesus in the storm and the stilling of the storm with reference to discipleship, and that means with reference to the little ship of the church."[1] Moreover, Matthew also transposes the words of rebuke to the disciples and the actual stilling of the storm. In Mark the miracle occurs first and the words of rebuke second; in Matthew the two episodes are reversed. "Before the elements are brought to silence, thus in the midst of a mortal threat, the word of Jesus goes forth to the disciples and puts them to shame for their little faith."[2] Moreover, not only is "men of little faith" a favorite expression of Matthew, but it also has a strong Jewish background and throughout Matthew's Gospel it is used frequently, as it is here, in the context of general discipleship. "Further, by the choice of this expression the special situation of the disciples, which in Mark is denoted by the question 'Have you no faith?' becomes a typical situation of discipleship as a whole."[3]

Bornkamm's article is the first work in what we are calling redaction criticism proper and we see in it the typical emphasis: Matthew is an interpreter of previous tradition and in his modifications of that tradition he reveals something of both his own theology and his evangelistic purpose. Bornkamm followed up this study with a more comprehensive one, which is also to be found in English in the Bornkamm, Barth, and

[1]Bornkamm in G. Bornkamm, G. Barth, H. J. Held, *Tradition and Interpretation in Matthew* (London: SCM; Philadelphia: Westminster, 1963), p. 55; hereafter cited as *Tradition and Interpretation*.
[2]*Ibid.*, p. 56.
[3]*Ibid.*

Held volume, and is there entitled "End-expectation and Church in Matthew." The results of this particular investigation in Matthew's Gospel were first announced at a meeting of theologians held in Germany on the fifth of January, 1954, where Bornkamm made a presentation, "Matthew as Interpreter of the Words of the Lord." The article embodying the complete investigation was first published (in German) in the volume of essays honoring C. H. Dodd.[4] We have called attention elsewhere to the irony of the fact that this first major publication of the new wave in New Testament studies initially appeared side by side in this volume with an article by T. W. Manson that attempted to stem the tide, namely, "The Life of Jesus: Some Tendencies in Present Day Research"![5]

Since Bornkamm's article is readily available in English we need spend no time here describing its contents in detail. It is sufficient for our purpose to point out that it is the first thoroughgoing redaction-critical investigation of the theological peculiarities and theme of Matthew's Gospel. As such it begins with the discourses into which Matthew arranges his presentation of the teaching of Jesus—discourses which, as has long been noted, exhibit something of the particular interest of Matthew as an author. Bornkamm shows how these discourses are shot through and through with a particular Matthean understanding of the church and its relationship to the imminent parousia. Then attention is given to the Matthean understanding of the Jewish Law and its role in Christian faith. From there Bornkamm turns to the Matthean Christology, which he approaches, quite properly, by means of that understanding of the relationship between Jesus himself and the Law which plays such an important role in the Matthean theology; in particular Bornkamm concerns himself with the various titles that Matthew uses in his presentation of his Christology. Finally, attention is given to the relationship between Christology and ecclesiology. The circle is complete and we return

[4]W. D. Davies and D. Daube (eds.), *The Background of the New Testament and its Eschatology. Studies in Honor of C. H. Dodd* (Cambridge: University Press, 1954, 1964).

[5]N. Perrin, "The *Wredestrasse* becomes the *Hauptstrasse*: Reflections on the Reprinting of the Dodd Festschrift," *Journal of Religion*, 46 (1966), 296–300.

to the role of the church, which is so prominent in the Matthean theology.[6]

Bornkamm's article is clearly the compressed result of a lengthy and detailed investigation of Matthew's Gospel; it is easily the most important statement made about the Matthean theology in many years; and it is the first presentation of the possibilities inherent in redaction criticism, a presentation so dramatic in its results that it opened the floodgates to the tide that was to follow.

Equally as important to our discipline as Bornkamm's own work is his role as teacher, for Bornkamm had a number of pupils whom he influenced to work along the lines which he himself had laid down in his two articles. He is fortunate in that a number of these pupils turned out to be first-class scholars in their own right and made contributions to the growth of redaction criticism which would be hard to over-estimate. Two of these, Gerhard Barth and Heinz Held, developed further the insights which are found in the two Born-kamm articles and grounded them more thoroughly in a detailed investigation of the material involved. Thus Barth wrote a dissertation on Matthew's understanding of the Law and Held produced one on Matthew as interpreter of the miracle stories. These two dissertations have now been translated into English and are presented in the Bornkamm, Barth, and Held volume to which reference has already so often been made. In addition to Barth and Held, Bornkamm had two other pupils who must here be noticed; indeed, their dissertations are major contributions to New Testament scholarship. These two are Heinz Eduard Tödt, author of *Son of Man in the Synoptic Tradition* and Ferdinand Hahn, author of *The Titles of Jesus in Christology*. A brief description of their work will be found in the Annotated Bibliography at the end of this book.

HANS CONZELMANN AND THE GOSPEL OF LUKE

If Günther Bornkamm is the first of the true redaction critics, Hans Conzelmann is certainly the most important. His *Theol-*

---

[6]G. Bornkamm, "End-expectation and Church in Matthew," *Tradition and Interpretation*, pp. 15–51.

ogy of St. Luke, first published in German in 1954, is the one
work above all others which focused attention upon this new
discipline and convinced a whole world of New Testament
scholarship that here, indeed, was a major new departure in
New Testament Studies. His book ranks with Bultmann's
History of the Synoptic Tradition or Jeremias's *The Parables of
Jesus* as one of the few truly seminal works of our time in the
field of New Testament research; neither the discipline of New
Testament theology as a whole nor the understanding of Luke
in particular will ever be the same again. Apart from the force
and power with which Conzelmann works, his impact is in
no small measure due to his decision to work on the Lucan
theology. Luke has generally been regarded by scholars as the
historian of early Christianity, and it is quite typical that an
important review of recent work on Luke by C. K. Barrett
should have the title *Luke the Historian in Recent Study.*[7]
Impressed by the accuracy of his references to officials in the
Roman Empire, by his obvious close acquaintanceship with the
customs and life of the empire, and by the vividness of his
narrative in Acts, the general tendency has been to see him as
the first church historian and to regard him as a much better
historian than many of those who followed him! With Conzelmann's accomplishment all this changes; Luke the historian
becomes a self-conscious theologian, and the details of his
composition can be shown convincingly to have been theologically motivated. To give but one example, the resurrection
appearances in the Lucan writings take place in Jerusalem in
contrast to the impression given elsewhere in the New Testament that they take place in Galilee. Conzelmann shows that
this geographical reference is not historical reminiscence, a
conclusion which raises questions as to the actual locale of
these appearances. Luke is in no way motivated by a desire
to exercise historical accuracy, but entirely by his theological
concept of the role of Jerusalem in the history of salvation.

Of Conzelmann, then, it may justifiably be said that he almost single-handedly changed the whole tenor of Lucan

[7]C. K. Barrett, *Luke the Historian in Recent Study* (London: Epworth
Press, 1961).

studies. It is symptomatic of the situation that C. H. Dodd, a representative of a more historicizing approach to the New Testament, should have written in a private letter, perhaps somewhat ruefully, "I suspect we shall have to give Acts over, so to speak, to Conzelmann."[8]

Working independently of others, Conzelmann begins his book by defining his approach to the material in terms of its contrast with both literary and form criticism. He notes, as by now we would expect, that literary criticism provides the fundamental basis upon which he works, namely, the theory—so important to him—of Luke's dependence upon Mark and Q. He goes on to say that form criticism had concerned itself with the smaller units and characteristically attempted to break off those units from their framework and to understand them in their most primitive form. He himself is concerned more with the framework and with later forms of the tradition. He attempts to understand what was happening to the tradition at those later stages and particularly, of course, at the stage represented by Luke:

> The first phase in the collection of the traditional material (up to the composition of Mark's gospel and the Q sayings) has been clarified by form criticism. Now a second phase has to be distinguished, in which the kerygma is not simply transmitted and received, but itself becomes the subject of reflection. This is what happens with Luke. This new stage is seen both in the critical attitude to tradition as well as in the positive formation of a new picture of history out of those already current, like stones used as parts of a new mosaic.[9]

The method which Conzelmann uses may be described somewhat as follows: He begins by carefully comparing the text of Luke with that of his source, mainly of course the Gospel of Mark, in order to determine what may be recognized as the Lucan editorial activity. Then he studies this activity as carefully as he can to determine what theological

[8]Quoted by R. R. Williams in D. E. Nineham *et al.*, *Historicity and Chronology in the New Testament* ("Theological Collections," No. 6 [London: SPCK, 1965]), p. 150.

[9]Conzelmann, *Theology of St. Luke*, trans. G. Buswell (New York: Harper & Row, 1960), p. 12.

motivation is to be seen at work in it, and he goes on from there to certain major texts which seem to him to summarize central aspects of the theological purpose he has detected in the editorial activity. Texts, for example, such as Luke 16:16 or Luke 13:31 ff., become keys for understanding the totality of the Lucan theological enterprise. Informed by the details he has learned from the minutiae of comparison and by the overall schema he has developed from the major Lucan texts, he goes on to analyze the totality of Luke-Acts in terms of how it reflects the Lucan theological purpose and expresses the Lucan theology. It must be stressed that the foundation upon which he builds is the careful and detailed comparison of the text of Luke with that of the sources Luke used, where these can be determined. This has to be emphasized because a superficial reading of Conzelmann's book might give the impression that he is putting too much weight upon a text such as Luke 16:16—indeed, this complaint has often been lodged against him by his critics. But the point is that he bases his dependence upon major texts upon the conviction that the ideas these texts express can be shown to have been the dominant factors behind Luke's many minor modifications of source material. On this detailed and thorough study of the Lucan modifications of his sources the whole enterprise of Conzelmann ultimately rests. Criticism of him can be valid only when it is built upon an equally detailed and thorough examination of the material, which is very rarely the case.

Conzelmann's presentation of the Lucan theology is by now very well-known and we need not discuss its details. He concentrates attention upon the *Heilsgeschichte* ("saving history") which Luke develops in three stages: stage one, the period of Israel to which John the Baptist belongs; stage two, the period of the ministry of Jesus which is "the center of time" (the actual title of Conzelmann's work in German) and which comes to an end with the ascension; stage three, the period of the church in the world during which one can look backward to the time of salvation and the ministry of Jesus, and forward to the parousia, which will bring this period to a close and will be the climax of all things. This scheme, Conzelmann argues, is Luke's response to the central theological problem of his day, namely, the delay of the parousia and the subsequent necessity for the church to come to terms with its continued and continuing existence in the world. Whereas at the beginning period the time of the church in the world was viewed as a brief interim very shortly to be brought to a close by the parousia, for Luke the time of the church in the world had to be regarded as indefinite. This created the problem to which his theological enterprise is a proposed solution. Luke's overall solution to the problem is reflected in the details of his theology and affects every aspect of his presentation of the ministry of Jesus and of the early church. One of the remarkable aspects of Conzelmann's work is not only that he shows how great the Lucan theological enterprise is in its conception, but also that he shows how detailed it is in its execution. For example, he is able to demonstrate that even such elements as geographical references in the Gospel story are made to reflect aspects of the Lucan theology: Galilee is the first place of the ministry of Jesus and here there is no temptation but only a manifestation of the time of salvation; Judea, especially Jerusalem, is the second place of the ministry of Jesus, but here there is temptation because here the passion occurs, and it is a necessary prelude to the resurrection and ascension. In this geographical scheme the ministry of John the Baptist does not belong to the time of salvation and hence is carefully separated in its locale from Galilee and Judea-Jerusalem, the places of Jesus. This is but one example of the detailed exposition which Conzelmann is able to make of the extent to which the Lucan theological enterprise has determined the smallest details of his narratives. As presented by Conzelmann, the theology of Luke is breathtaking both in the grandeur of its conception and in the careful detail of its application and exposition in narrative form. It is no wonder that since Conzelmann's work, attention has been concentrated upon Luke as theologian rather than as historian, or if as historian, then historian understood in a very special way, as we pointed out above. Indeed, not the least of the benefits which redaction criticism has conferred upon us is this sudden reve-

lation of Luke as a major theologian of early Christianity.
What is more, it turns out that Luke himself was wrestling in
his way with a problem which greatly concerns the theologians
of today, namely the problem of faith and history in general,
and the "question of the historial Jesus" in particular!

WILLI MARXSEN AND THE GOSPEL OF MARK

The third of the redaction critics proper, as we are calling
them, is Willi Marxsen whose book *Der Evangelist Markus*
(English translation: *Mark the Evangelist* [1969]) was first
published in 1956. It consists of four redaction-critical studies
of the Gospel of Mark which were originally presented to the
University of Kiel in 1954 as a *Habilitationsschrift*[10] and were
therefore carried out quite independently of the work of Bornkamm or Conzelmann. Indeed, in the prologue to the book
Marxsen notes that he was working along the same lines as
Conzelmann because redaction criticism was "in the air" after
the Second World War just as form criticism was after the
First.

As we have already said, Marxsen is responsible for the
name *Redaktionsgeschichte*, which we are representing as redaction criticism. His book begins with a systematic consideration of the new methodology and its relationship to form
criticism, and it is here that he proposes the term *Redaktionsgeschichte*. In this systematic presentation Marxsen contrasts
redaction criticism with form criticism at four points. First,
he stresses the difference between the understanding of the
evangelists in the one discipline and the other. Form criticism
regarded the evangelists primarily as collectors of tradition,
whereas redaction criticism regards them as authors in their
own right. Secondly, form criticism was mostly concerned
with breaking down the tradition into small units and particularly with the way in which these small units came into being

[10]The German academician in effect writes two doctoral theses. The
first of these is his *Promotion*, roughly equivalent to the English language
Ph.D.; the second is his *Habilitation*, to which the English language
academic world has no equivalent. The *Habilitation* is necessary for a
German before it is permissible for him to hold a professorial chair
at a university.

in the first place. Redaction criticism, however, concerns itself with the larger units down to and including the particular form of Gospel and asks questions about the purpose of the formation of these larger units of tradition. Thirdly, form criticism with its concern for the individual units of tradition and its understanding of the evangelists as collectors of tradition could never do justice to that bold new step taken by the evangelist Mark, who gathers together individual units and larger collections of tradition and out of them fashions something wholly new—a "Gospel." Both Matthew and Luke inherit this form, "Gospel," from Mark and make further use of it themselves; in no small measure it is the purpose of redaction criticism to do justice to both the Marcan theology lying behind the creation of the form "Gospel" and to those aspects of the Lucan and Matthean theology which become evident as we consider the way in which they use the form as well as the tradition which they inherit from Mark. Fourthly, in keeping with his understanding of the totality of the transmission of tradition from its creation in the early church to its reformulation by the synoptic evangelists, Marxsen claims that one should be prepared to consider three separate "settings-in-life" for synoptic tradition. If one is prepared to follow Joachim Jeremias in his work on the parables and claim a setting in the life of Jesus for a certain amount of the synoptic material, then one also has to follow the form critics and consider a setting in the life of the early church for the tradition created and transmitted there, and then finally one has to consider the setting in the purpose or theology of the evangelist. This last setting is the concern of redaction criticism. The idea of a threefold *Sitz im Leben* is a most important conception and one to which we have called attention elsewhere.[11] It will come to play an increasing part in future New Testament studies, and the only problem is that of finding an appropriate terminology. The present tendency is to have something of a mixture of German, Latin, and English. We propose, therefore, the following three terms: (1) setting in the life of Jesus; (2) setting in the life and work of the

[11] N. Perrin, *Rediscovering the Teaching of Jesus*, p. 256.

early church; (3) setting in the work and purpose of the evangelist. We shall use these terms ourselves from now on and we hope that either these or some other appropriate ones will become established as the way to refer to these most definite realities of early Christian tradition.

Marxsen's statement sums up the things that we have been saying about redaction criticism. We wish to modify it merely to the extent that redaction criticism not only considers the work of the evangelists as we have them, but also the work of any creator of a new unit of tradition in which a theological viewpoint is expressed, meaning particularly the sayings source Q upon which Tödt has done excellent work. Marxsen himself, of course, would be the first to agree with this, and doubtless would have said so had he written his Introduction later than he did.

The four studies which make up the body of Marxsen's book are independent of one another, but they have a common theme in that they are all concerned with an aspect of the Marcan theology as revealed in the particular subject matter under discussion and then with the way in which the re-use of the Marcan material by Matthew and Luke reflects aspects of the Matthean and Lucan theologies respectively. In this way Marxsen deals with (1) the tradition concerning John the Baptist, (2) geographical references in the Gospel narratives, (3) the conception *euangelion* (Gospel), (4) Mark 13. We cannot here give a summary of the contents of the book, nor can we enter into discussion with Marxsen about any of the points he makes; however, we shall indicate something of his method by offering a sample from his discussion of the John the Baptist tradition, and we shall also refer to a major point he makes which actually implies a new departure within redaction criticism and indicates a possible way forward to the future. First, then, a sample of his work.

Marxsen begins his study of the John the Baptist tradition by describing the way it is used by the evangelist Mark. He argues that, whatever the case may be with regard to the elements of previous tradition that Mark is using, in the form in which it is presented in the Gospel of Mark the tradition is

35

a Marcan composition, and as such it can tell us a good deal
about the Marcan theology. Mark has in fact composed
"backwards"; his purpose is to interpret the story of Jesus by
means of this reference to John the Baptist. The John the Baptist tradition is presented not because of any particular historical interest in the Baptist nor because of any desire to say
how things actually were, but because Mark wants to use this
tradition to say something about Jesus. "What comes before
(i.e. the story of the Baptist) is presented from the viewpoint
of what was to come after (i.e. the story of Jesus). That means,
however: the Baptist does not have any independent significance of his own; there can be no teaching about the Baptist
or about baptism; rather, all that is said about the Baptist is
in effect something said about the Christ."[12] But one can go
even further than this, for just as the Baptist interprets Jesus,
so the quotations from the Old Testament incorporated in
the narrative interpret the Baptist himself. The juxtaposition
of the Old Testament prophecies concerning the wilderness
in Mark 1:3 and the appearance of John the Baptist in the
wilderness in verse 4 shows us that John the Baptist is here
being interpreted as the fulfiller of these prophecies and, as
such, as the forerunner of Jesus. But this means that the reference to the wilderness in verse 4, whatever may have been
its origins in the tradition, is not a geographical reference at
all, but is rather a theological statement.

The wilderness is not a geographical location. It is not permissible to reflect as to where it could lie. This reference is not
intended to give a location for the work of the Baptist . . . rather
"in the wilderness" qualifies the Baptist as the one who fulfills
Old Testament prophecy. It might almost be said: The Baptist
would even be the one who came "in the desert," even if in his
whole life he had never once been anywhere near the desert.[13]

Similarly with the references to time: Although verse 14
certainly refers to the arrest of John the Baptist by Herod, it
does not necessarily indicate that the ministry of Jesus began
only after John had been arrested. In its present place it

---

[12]Marxsen, *Der Evangelist Markus*, p. 19 (Eng. trans., p. 33).
[13]*Ibid.*, p. 22 (Eng. trans., pp. 37 f.).

simply means that, theologically speaking, John was the forerunner and Jesus the one who came after; hence, the story of
John has to be brought to an end before the story of Jesus can
properly begin, and it is for this reason that John is "delivered
up" in verse 14. The actual story of the arrest and death of
John the Baptist will be given later in the Gospel, but the
reference to the arrest has to come also in verse 14 because
of the evangelist's desire to relate John the Baptist and Jesus
theologically. So Mark can have in verse 1 "the beginning of
the gospel of Jesus Christ" quite properly because the story of
John the Baptist is, theologically speaking, the story of the
forerunner of Jesus. Thus by a presentation of his story a
beginning can be made to the interpretation of Jesus as the
Christ, which is a major purpose of the whole Gospel.

Having discussed the use of the Baptist tradition by Mark,
Marxsen goes on to discuss the use of the Marcan form of this
tradition by Matthew and Luke. He points out, for example,
that the reference to the wilderness (in Mark a theological
statement) becomes in Matthew and Luke a geographical one.
For Matthew the reference to the Old Testament takes on
new force and meaning, as indeed do references to the Old
Testament throughout his Gospel. He reflects on these far more
than does Mark and sees them not only as a means of interpreting the New Testament story, in this instance that of John
the Baptist, but also as the very ground for there being such
a story to interpret. So for him the Old Testament is not only
the means for interpreting the New, but also its prehistory.
Further in this direction, Matthew has taken the theological
ordering of the relationship between John the Baptist and
Jesus in Mark and made it a chronological ordering. In the
Gospel of Luke this tendency to order John the Baptist and
Jesus chronologically is carried still further, and Luke actually
separates the story of John the Baptist from that of Jesus in
a way which Matthew does not. Luke relegates the Baptist
to the Jewish prehistory of the Gospel and does not—as Mark
does—see the story of the Baptist as part of the Gospel story.
Thus the ministry of the Baptist is, theologically speaking, regarded as being at an end before the baptism of Jesus even

37

takes place. Thus, too, Luke relates the account of the arrest of John *before* he gives any account of the baptism of Jesus and, in his account of the baptism, the figure of John almost disappears. For Luke, the Baptist no longer has eschatological but only historical significance; he is a prophet belonging to that period of the prophets which came to an end with the coming of Jesus.[14] In this way Marxsen investigates the three accounts of the Baptist in the synoptic Gospels and shows that, although these accounts have only small differences from a literary standpoint, these differences are indicative of major variations in theological conception.

Although Marxsen's four studies are conceived and carried out independently of one another, they all relate to the Marcan theology. Each reflects in one way or another a central point about that theology, a point which to Marxsen is very important. In thus carrying redaction criticism to its furthest limit Marxsen perhaps points the way to a still future day and work. This new departure is his conception that the Marcan theology reflects the situation in Galilee in the year 66 A.D. at the beginning of the Jewish War against Rome. Marxsen believes that the Christian community of Jerusalem had fled from Jerusalem to Galilee at the beginning of the war, that there they were waiting for the parousia which they believed to be imminent. The Gospel of Mark, claims Marxsen, reflects this situation in its theology. So, for example, the present ending of the Gospel at 16:8 is the true ending; Mark did not intend to go on to report resurrection appearances in Galilee; the references to Galilee in 14:28 and 16:7 are not references to the resurrection at all but to the parousia. There never was, therefore, an ending to the Gospel in which Mark reported resurrection appearances in Galilee. The "you will see him" in 16:7 is a reference to the parousia and to the future. But Mark expects this event to take place immediately, in his own day. The parousia has not yet come but it is now imminent.[15] This is an argument from Marxsen's discussion of the geo-

---

[14]*Ibid.*, p. 31 (Eng. trans., p. 51), where he relates his views to those of Conzelmann.
[15]*Ibid.*, p. 54 (Eng. trans., p. 85).

graphical references in the Gospel, but similarly in his study of Mark 13 we find the same situation envisaged. He interprets Mark 13 as a totality and does not concern himself with the question of the traditional material that may have been brought together in it, since he correctly sees that the final form of the chapter will be representative of the Marcan theological position. So he claims that we can determine a good deal about the time and place of the composition of this chapter from the chapter itself. We will concern ourselves with only one of his arguments, namely the argument based on Mark 13:14: "But when you see the desolating sacrilege set up where it ought not to be (let the reader understand), then let those who are in Judea flee to the mountains." We have in this verse a reference to the actual situation of the Christian community in Jerusalem which fled into the mountains of Galilee at the threat inherent in the outbreak of the Jewish War. In this understanding of the verse the parenthesis "let the reader understand" is Mark's way of directing his readers from their present situation in Galilee to the eschatological future they are expecting.

It is not our purpose here to defend or to debate with Marxsen the correctness of his insight with regard to the place and time of the composition of Mark's Gospel. Our concern is to point out that here we are moving beyond redaction criticism itself to a still newer stage, a stage in which we work from a theological insight we have been able to determine to the historical situation in which that insight arose. This is the direction in which our studies ultimately will move; certainly the challenge would seem to be appropriate. If redaction criticism helps us to determine more and more exactly the theological developments in earliest Christianity, then it will be natural for us to go on to ask ourselves what historical circumstances lie behind these theological developments. It may well be then that redaction criticism itself will ultimately produce a theological history of earliest Christianity such as it has not yet been possible to write.

III

Redaction Criticism at
Work: A Sample

THE INCIDENT AT CAESAREA PHILIPPI

In this chapter we give an example of the kind of thing
redaction criticism does, and in this way we hope to help the
discipline come alive for the reader. We have chosen the account of the incident at Caesarea Philippi, the story concerning the confession of Peter and the subsequent teaching of
Jesus on discipleship (Mark 8:27–9:1 with its parallels, Matt.
16:13–28 and Luke 9:18–27), because this story has always
played a large part in any attempt to reconstruct a life of Jesus.
In this example, therefore, the differences between a redaction-critical approach and the older way of regarding it as
essentially a historical narrative will be most evident.

At this point we pause to make it clear that we are not
concerned here with arguing the case for redaction criticism as
an approach to the Gospels in general or to this narrative in
particular. The evidence and arguments which led the present
writer to adopt form criticism and redaction criticism as the
only legitimate approach to the Gospel narratives were set
out in N. Perrin, *Rediscovering the Teaching of Jesus*, pp. 15–
32, and there is no point in repeating them here. So far as this
particular narrative is concerned, the way that redaction criticism is able to make sense of the phenomena demonstrably
present in the texts is itself a validation of the methodology.

THE MARCAN NARRATIVE: MARK 8:27–9:1

The Marcan narrative has a remarkably clear structure and it should first be read in its entirety, with the reader resolutely leaving to one side any reminiscences of the Matthean or Lucan parallels and even more resolutely banishing from his mind reminiscences of lives of Jesus that he may have read. When we do this we arrive at the following general picture. Jesus and his disciples are on a journey from Bethsaida to some villages in the region of Caesarea Philippi and he asks them the double question: Who do men say . . . Who do you say that I am? They reply with a statement that represents the general opinion (such as Mark had already used in 6:14 f.), and then, through the mouth of Peter, with the fundamental confession of early Christianity: "You are the Christ." Jesus accepts this and charges them to keep it from anyone else, and he then goes on to teach them concerning the coming suffering of the Son of man (note: "Son of man," not "Christ"). Peter vehemently rejects this teaching, and Jesus, with an eye to the disciples as a group, in turn reprimands Peter in the strongest possible terms, identifying him in this moment as Satan. This dispute with Peter leads to a second block of teaching by Jesus, this time directed to the crowd as well as to the disciples, indicating that the disciple must be prepared to accept the possibility of martyrdom as the price of his discipleship. The narrative then reaches its climax in two sayings: the first issues a stern warning that those who fail the Son of man in the hour of trial will rue it at the Last Judgment; and the second offers a reassuring promise that those who stand firm will be delivered by the coming of the kingdom "in power."

Reading the narrative by itself in this way, one cannot help but be struck by a number of distinctive features. In particular there is the remarkable way in which the action moves backwards and forwards between the historical situation of the ministry of Jesus and the historical situation of the church for which Mark is writing. The reply to the first question refers to

41

opinions available in the Palestinian situation of the ministry of Jesus, but the second block of teaching, in its present form. uses language derived from the situation of the early church ("take up his cross," " . . . and the gospel's"). The questions, answers, and teaching are on the lips of Jesus and Peter, but the titles involved are from the christological vocabulary of the early church. Further in this direction, we must note that, although the characters in the pericope bear names or designations derived from the circumstances of the ministry (i.e., "Jesus," "Peter," "the multitude"), they also equally represent the circumstances of the early church: "Jesus" is the Lord addressing his church, "Peter" represents fallible believers who confess correctly yet go on to interpret their confession incorrectly, and "the multitude" is the whole church membership for whom the general teaching which follows is designed. So we come to the all-important point so far as a redaction-critical view of the narrative is concerned: it has the form of a story about the historical Jesus and his disciples but a purpose in terms of the risen Lord and his church. Moreover, this purpose is a specifically Marcan purpose; it represents Mark's understanding of what the risen Lord has to say to the church of his day.

The fundamental premise of redaction criticism, then, is that the pericope can be analyzed from the perspective of a Marcan purpose. The goal of such an analysis is to understand the purpose and the theology that is revealed in the purpose. To this end we concern ourselves both with the individual parts of the narrative and with the story as a whole. In other words, we analyze the constituent parts of the narrative, such as the sayings, etc., to see what they tell us of Mark as one who gathers, modifies, or creates tradition, and we analyze the total narrative in terms of its overall purposes, such as its setting in the framework of the Gospel as a whole, etc., to see what this will tell us about Mark as an evangelist.

We shall begin with a discussion of four constituent parts of this narrative: the prediction of the passion (8:31); the teaching about discipleship (8:34–37); the climactic warning (8:38); and the climactic promise (9:1). In each case we shall raise the question of the previous history of the material in the tradition in order to set the stage for a consideration of the Marcan redactional work upon that material, and then we shall discuss both the redaction of the material by Mark and also the particular use which he has made of it.

THE PREDICTION OF THE PASSION: MARK 8:31

And he began to teach them that the Son of man must suffer many things, and be rejected by the elders and the chief priests and the scribes, and be killed, and after three days rise again.

This is one of three passion predictions in Mark (8:31; 9:31; 10:33 f.). These sayings have such a complex history in the tradition that it is beyond our present capacity to unravel it in its details. This complexity is really what we should expect, for the problem of the crucified Messiah was the major problem for the early church, both in terms of the development of her own theology and of the development of an apologetic to Judaism, and she brought her every theological resource to bear upon it. The result of the church's wrestling with this problem is that the traditions that crystallized out of her struggle bear the marks of many different factors (use of various Old Testament passages in exegesis and "passion apologetic" [B. Lindars], a speculative Son of man theology, a development of a doctrine of divine necessity, emphasis upon the cross as redemptive and/or the resurrection as decisive victory, etc.). It is a task beyond our current resources to analyze these factors in their entirety, although we are increasingly developing insights into various parts of the tradition they represent.[1]

In this particular instance, therefore, we cannot learn anything about Mark and his theology from his redaction of tradition, but the matter is far different with regard to his use of

---

[1]The two most important recent discussions are H. E. Tödt, *The Son of Man in the Synoptic Tradition*, trans. Dorothea M. Barton (Philadelphia: Westminster Press, 1965), pp. 141–221, hereafter cited as *Son of Man;* and B. Lindars, *New Testament Apologetic*, (Philadelphia: Westminster Press, 1962), pp. 75–137. The present writer proposes to approach the problem of the suffering Son of man sayings at a later date in light of the insights and arguments of N. Perrin, *Rediscovering the Teaching of Jesus*, pp. 164–99.

it. Following in part Tödt's excellent analysis of this aspect of the Marcan theological purpose,[2] we note that the section of the Gospel 8:27–10:52 serves to introduce the passion narrative and to prepare the reader to understand it correctly. It presents to the reader the Marcan theological understanding of the cross; to use our own words, it offers a theological treatise on the meaning of the cross in narrative form. The section is a carefully composed unit held together by three geographical references: 8:27, ". . . to the villages of Caesarea Philippi" (north of Galilee); 9:30, ". . . from there and passed through Galilee"; 10:1, ". . . he left there and went to the region of Judea and beyond the Jordan" (i.e., he moves toward Jerusalem). Each of these three divisions of the unit has its own passion prediction (8:31; 9:31; 10:33 f.), and the dramatic tension is heightened by the fact that the last one includes a specific reference to the Jerusalem toward which the group is moving as the locale of the passion (Mark himself must be responsible for this aspect of the saying). So we learn from the sayings themselves, and from their function in the composition of the Gospel, something of the Marcan theology of the cross. Since we cannot isolate the Marcan redactional elements in the sayings themselves, we cannot determine how much of this theology is specifically Marcan and how much general early Christian, but the boldness of conception and the effectiveness of execution in presenting it in this narrative form is remarkable.

THE TEACHING ABOUT DISCIPLESHIP: MARK 8:34–37

And he called to him the multitude with his disciples, and said to them, "If any man would come after me, let him deny himself and take up his cross and follow me. For whoever would save his life will lose it; and whoever loses his life for my sake and the gospel's will save it. For what does it profit a man, to gain the whole world and forfeit his life? For what can a man give in return for his life?"

This section is made up of four sayings which very likely originally circulated separately in the tradition and then were

*Tödt, *Son of Man,* pp. 144–49.

44

gradually brought together because of their similarity of content and because of the common catchword "life." In the parallel passage in Matthew (16:24–26) all four sayings appear; in Luke (9:23–25) only the first three; in addition Matthew has versions of the first two joined together at his 10:38 f. and Luke has versions of them separately at his 14:27 and 17:33. Mark's verses 36 and 37 are found in Matthew and Luke only where they are following Mark (Luke omits verse 37), but they must have originally been separate sayings because they make quite different points: verse 36 that riches are of no avail at death and verse 37 that life is the highest good (Bultmann). So Mark has brought together a group of sayings which originally circulated separately, but in doing this he is only completing a process that was already going on in the tradition. In itself this is common editorial activity in the tradition and of no more theological significance for Mark than for the anonymous editors of the tradition who preceded him. However, the Marcan activity in introducing a group of sayings on the cost of discipleship at this particular point in the narrative does serve a definite theological purpose: it reflects the Marcan conviction that, as went the master, so must go the disciple, with all that this implies theologically. That this is definitely the result of deliberate editorial activity can be seen from the fact that it happens in each instance of a passion prediction and, moreover, there is a constant editorial pattern of prediction–misunderstanding–teaching: so in 8:31, passion prediction; 8:32 f., dispute between Jesus and Peter; 8:34–37, teaching about discipleship; and again, in 9:31, passion prediction; 9:33 f., report of a dispute about greatness; 9:35–37, teaching; and finally, 10:33 f., passion prediction; 10:35–41, request of James and John arising out of their misunderstanding of the nature of glory; 10:42–45, teaching. Furthermore, the three sets of teaching are carefully related to one another in content so as to make a total impact and to develop a total theological point. In the first one the disciple must be prepared to take up his cross, as did the master; in the second he must imitate the master in servanthood; in the third that servanthood is defined in a saying which both takes up

45

the previous themes of cross and servanthood and presents these aspects of the Marcan theology in all their fullness: "For the Son of man also came not to be served but to serve, and to give his life as a ransom for many." The boldness and effectiveness of this method of stating a theme and developing an exhortation based upon it must again be described as remarkable.

THE CLIMACTIC WARNING: MARK 8:38

For whoever is ashamed of me and of my words in this adulterous and sinful generation, of him will the Son of man also be ashamed, when he comes in the glory of his Father with the holy angels.

This saying has a history in the tradition prior to Mark which can be traced with comparative certainty.[3] In its very earliest form it probably ran (in Aramaic): "Everyone who acknowledges me before man, he will be acknowledged before the angels of God." It was taken up into that tradition of the early church which was concerned with the pronouncement of judgment upon offenders, which judgment however would be carried out by God at the *eschaton* (end time).[4] It was then translated into Greek and came to be known in the variety of versions which can be detected in Matthew 10:32 f. and parallel passage, Luke 12:8 f.:

So every one who acknowledges me before men, I (Luke: the Son of man) also will acknowledge before my Father who is in heaven (Luke: the angels of God); but whoever denies me before men, I also will deny before my Father who is in heaven (Luke: will be denied before the angels of God).

Here the important points to note are that the saying has become a double saying using the verbs "acknowledge" and "deny," and that the subject of the action in the second clause can now either be "I" or "the Son of man" or God (when the

---

[3]We are now summarizing what we argued in detail in Perrin, *Rediscovering*, pp. 185–91, with the difference that we are not here concerned, as we were there, with the question as to whether any form of the saying can be held to go back to Jesus himself.

[4]On this tradition, brilliantly isolated by Käsemann on form-critical grounds, see Perrin, *Rediscovering*, pp. 22 f.

verb is in the passive). It must have been in some such version that Mark knew the saying, and the changes from this earlier version to the version in Mark 8:38 are due to Marcan redaction.

In the tradition from which the saying comes, the emphasis was upon the future judgment of God, and a specific form was created to express this judgment, namely, the form of a two-part sentence with the same verb in each part, expressing in the first part the activity being judged and in the second the nature of the judgment. This act of pronouncing judgment was carried out at the Eucharist and the form used for it came to be widely used in early Christian exhortation, no doubt because it carried with it something of the aura of that moment of solemn judgment at the Eucharist. It must have been for this reason that Mark chooses to use the form here. Intending this as the climactic warning of the pericope, he deliberately chooses a form which for his readers will strike the chord of the solemn judgment pronouncement of the church.

The changes in the actual saying from the version(s) detectable in Matthew 10:32 f. and parallel passages are similarly reflective of the Marcan purpose. The two most important of these changes are the generalizing of the specific double emphasis "acknowledge-deny" into the single "be ashamed,"[5] and the choice of "Son of man" to express the subject of the second clause rather than either of the other possibilities presented by the tradition, i.e., the first personal pronoun or the passive voice (the latter as a circumlocution for "God"). The first of these changes is due to the fact that the saying is now the warning part of a double climax of warning and promise (the promise being found in Mark 9:1) and so needs to become a single warning saying to balance the second saying, the promise. A double saying including both promise and warning would clearly be unbalanced when linked with a single saying expressing promise. The choice of "Son of man" has a

[5]On the details of the development of this tradition and for the arguments supporting the assertion made here, see Perrin, *Rediscovering*, pp. 185–99.

double ground. On the one hand it makes a very effective combination to balance "Son of man" in the warning against "kingdom of God" in the promise, and on the other hand the use of "Son of man" here naturally recalls the "Son of man" in 8:31 (where, it should be noted, "Son of man" is introduced rather abruptly since "Christ" is actually the title upon which the contextual discussion turns). By means of this juxtaposition Mark is able to make the christological point that the one whose cross is the example to be followed is also the one whose coming in judgment is to be anticipated. In this context we may note that the use of the verb "ashamed" becomes very effective indeed, a point which provides another reason for regarding this version of the saying as a Marcan product.

THE CLIMACTIC PROMISE: MARK 9:1

And he said to them, "Truly, I say to you, there are some standing here who will not taste death before they see the kingdom of God come with power."

The present writer has wrestled with this saying throughout his academic career and during the course of some ten years of work his opinion has moved from holding it to be a genuine saying of Jesus to accepting that it is a Marcan product.[6] To summarize what we have argued in more detail elsewhere, there are a number of features about the saying which call for an explanation: it has distinctively Marcan characteristics, and it is related in form to Mark 13:30 as it is in content to Mark 8:38. We shall discuss these matters in turn.

The Marcan characteristics are the reference to "seeing" the parousia and the use of the words "power" and "glory" in this kind of context. Mark speaks of seeing the parousia here in 9:1, again in 13:26, and for a third time in 14:62. Matthew follows Mark on each occasion (Matt. 16:28; 24:30; 26:64), but he never uses the verb "to see" in connection with

[6]The changes and developments in the writer's opinion can be traced through the successive works, N. Perrin, *The Kingdom of God in the Teaching of Jesus* (Philadelphia: Westminster Press, 1963), *passim* [see refs. to Mark 9:1 in the Index]) and *Rediscovering*, pp. 16–20, 199–201.

the parousia elsewhere in his Gospel. Luke transforms Mark 9:1 into a non-parousia reference, as we shall argue below, and he follows Mark 13:26 (Luke 21:27), but he omits the reference to seeing in his version of Mark 14:62 (Luke 22:69). Luke, like Matthew, also has no such usage except in dependence on Mark. Mark uses "power" and "glory" in a parousia context in 8:38 ("glory") and 9:1 ("power"). Both Matthew (16:27 f.) and Luke (9:26 f.) follow him with regard to the use of "glory" but omit the reference to "power." Mark 10:37 has "in your glory" with reference to the parousia, Matthew (20:21) changes this to "in your kingdom"; Luke has no parallel. Mark 13:26 speaks of the Son of man "coming with great power and glory"; Matthew (24:30) and Luke (21:27) both follow this. Luke has no such usage elsewhere and Matthew only one, Matthew 25:31, which is the beginning of the parable of the sheep and the goats: "When the Son of man comes in his glory, and all the angels with him, then he will sit on his glorious throne." In view of Matthew 19:28, ". . . in the new world, when the Son of man shall sit on his glorious throne" (no parallels), this looks like a combination of Marcan and Matthean characteristics.

The relationship between Mark 9:1 and 13:30 in form and content is as follows: (1) Both begin with the identical solemn asseveration, "Truly, I say to you." (2) Both continue with a promise that is similar in content (9:1, ". . . there are some standing here who will not taste death before they see the kingdom of God come with power"; 13:30, ". . . this generation will not pass away before all these things take place") and exactly parallel in form. Both use in the Greek a clause introduced by *hoti* and both express the negation by the use of double negative with the subjunctive. (3) Both relate the promise to the coming of the eschaton.

The best explanation for this combination of data is the supposition that Mark himself has composed his 9:1 using the saying he has in his 13:30 as a model. Verse 13:30 itself is almost certainly non-Marcan. It is a general piece of Jewish Christian apocalyptic which has non-Marcan linguistic characteristics, and it fits its present context so very closely (it

49

finally answers the question which introduces the apocalyptic discourse, 13:5–27, and the "these things" clearly are the things referred to in that discourse) that there can be little doubt but that the apocalyptic seer (neither Jesus nor Mark!) who is responsible for this discourse composed 13:30 in order to bring his discourse to an end.[7] With this as a model Mark has varied the content of the affirmation but not the form, adopting for his purpose some stock phraseology from Jewish apocalyptic. (Compare IV Ezra 6:25 f.: "And it shall be whosoever shall have survived all these things that I have foretold unto thee, he shall be saved and shall see my salvation. . . . And the men who have been taken up, who have not tasted death from their birth, shall appear.") The promise itself varies in content from 13:30 in that it is expressed in terms of the kingdom's coming in power. The use of "kingdom of God" in this context is undoubtedly due to the fact that such a usage is a feature of the Jesus tradition itself. As Mark had gone to Jewish apocalyptic for the raw materials of the first part of this saying, so he has gone to the tradition of the sayings of Jesus for those of the second part. He will have been motivated in part by the fact that in the Jesus tradition "the kingdom of God" is most often used in a context of promise or blessing. So it will have been natural for him to construct a kingdom saying in the form of a promise to balance the use of "Son of man" in the preceding warning. But although this kind of use of "kingdom of God," and of the verb "to come," were characteristic of the Jesus tradition, and, for that matter, of Jesus himself, both the tense of the verb (the perfect) and the phrase "in power" are Marcan. To put the verb in the perfect and to add "in power" is to stress the promise as a promise for an experience of

[7] We would reject the suggestion made, for example, by V. Taylor, *The Gospel According to St. Mark* (New York: St. Martin's Press, 1952), p. 521, that this saying was originally a genuine saying of Jesus referring to the destruction of Jerusalem which "has been adapted in the interests of contemporary apocalyptic." This is an ingenious attempt to salvage the saying as a genuine word of Jesus, but there is not one shred of evidence that the saying ever existed in a form other than that which it now has. See further, Perrin, *Rediscovering*, p. 200.

complete fulfillment, all of which comes naturally in a saying intended as the climactic promise of a whole pericope.

We have spent some time on the arguments for the Marcan authorship of this particular saying because this is an important example of one kind of redactional possibility, namely, free composition by the redactor on the basis of traditional materials of various kinds. Indeed, one reason for choosing this narrative as an example is that within its comparatively brief compass we have instances of three distinct redactional possibilities: (1) the bringing together of previously existing independent sayings or shorter combinations of sayings (8: 36–7); (2) the modification of a saying in an existing tradition of the church (8:38); (3) the creation of a new saying using materials already present in the traditions of the church and of Jewish apocalyptic.

So Mark 9:1 is a climactic promise constructed by Mark himself to bring to an end this dramatic incident. It balances the warning of the preceding saying and ends the whole on a note of assurance, an assurance expressed in the strongest terms which the traditions inherited by Mark could offer or which Mark could conceive.[8] A discussion of the exact meaning indicated by Mark in this assurance must wait until we have viewed the narrative as a whole from the perspective of Mark's intention, to which we now turn.

THE NARRATIVE AS A WHOLE

Having discussed in some detail four individual parts of the Caesarea Philippi narrative in Mark, we now must consider the narrative again in its entirety. When we do this, one thing noticeable is the very strong emphasis upon persecution and suffering. The Son of man "must suffer many

[8] We have spoken of Mark throughout as a self-conscious—one might even say cold-blooded!—editor, redactor, and author. We should perhaps stress the obvious fact that this is simply a scholarly convenience as we discuss what he did, and it is not meant to prejudge any questions with regard to inspiration, sense of having "the mind of the Lord," view of the tradition and its relationship to Jesus, etc. But before any such questions can be discussed, it is essential to be clear as to what Mark in fact did, and to determine this is, in part, the purpose of redaction criticism.

things," the disciple must "deny himself and take up his cross"; there is the ever-present possibility of saving one's life only to lose it, of losing it only to save it, and so on. Moreover, as we noted earlier, the whole moves in a most remarkable manner between the historical situation of the ministry of Jesus and that of the early church, and it is quite evident that the pericope is concerned both with the sufferings of Jesus as Son of man on the one hand and with the potential sufferings of Christians "for my sake and the gospel's" on the other. The narrative presupposes a context of formal persecution for the readers. Recognizing this to be the case, a major purpose of the narrative then becomes apparent: the author is concerned with preparing the readers for that persecution by linking it backwards with the sufferings of Jesus and forwards with their own ultimate destiny. On the one hand, as went the Master, so must go the disciple; on the other, as goes the disciple now, so will go the Master with him at the End.

In a very real sense, therefore, this pericope is a tract for the times, and the times are those of formal persecution of Christians as Christians. We cannot now reconstruct the historical situation of the church to which Mark is addressing himself in the sense that we can name the Roman city or emperor concerned, but we can say that it is a situation in which persecution is a very real possibility and that preparation of his readers for this possibility is a very real part of the Marcan purpose.

If we turn next to a consideration of the narrative in its setting in the Gospel as a whole, then the first and most obvious thing to be noted is the fact that has been so often noted: this narrative is the watershed of the Gospel. Lives of Jesus without number have been built upon the supposition that there was a "Galilean springtime" in the ministry of Jesus, that this was followed by a darkening "via dolorosa" which led to Calvary, and that the transition from the one to the other came at Caesarea Philippi. That this supposition has so long endured is mute testimony to the skill of Mark as an author for, as we pointed out earlier, this narrative is certainly designed by him to introduce his particular theology of the cross. That he chose to do this in the form of narrative rather than theological treatise is his business; that his work has had such a tremendous impact upon subsequent generations is testimony to the effectiveness of his choice. A Marcan treatise on the cross might even have earned an honored place in the library of Christian theological literature, but the Marcan schematization of the ministry of Jesus has become part of the lifeblood of Christian devotional thinking. It is perhaps not out of place to add that the validity of the Marcan presentation is not dependent upon whether Caesarea Philippi "actually happened" but upon the meaningfulness of the cross as presented to Christian devotion in this way.

It is not our present purpose to summarize the Marcan theology of the cross presented in this pericope and subsequently through his Gospel. In our view Mark is a significant and creative literary figure and deserves to be read in the form in which he chose to write rather than in summary. Mark has the right to be read on his own terms, and after several generations of being read mistakenly, as a historian, he has earned the right to be read as a theologian. The reader is therefore invited to consider for himself the text of Mark and the theology of the cross which it presents. Our purpose is simply to point out that, from the viewpoint of redaction criticism, this is one way in which the text should be read.

A further emphasis in this narrative is that of Christology, and in this connection the narrative has a number of notable features. In the first place, we should notice that it uses the title "Christ": "Peter answered him, 'You are the Christ'" (8:29). At first sight this is by no means remarkable, for Peter is here formally representing the early church and therefore appropriately using the confessional title used by that church. But if we look at the Gospel as a whole, then we can see that, in general, the way Mark uses "Christ" focuses attention very sharply upon its use in this particular incident. The title occurs only seven times in Mark: 1:1; 8:29;

53

9:41; 12:35; 13:21; 14:61; 15:32. Of these seven instances one (9:41) is simply a way of saying "Christian," four (12: 35; 13:21; 14:61; 15:32) are references to "the anointed one" of Jewish messianic expectation, and one (1:1) is clearly a part of the formal superscription to the Gospel as a whole. This throws the last one (8:29) into very strong relief and demands of us that we pay due attention to the fact that only here in the Gospel of Mark is Jesus formally acknowledged as the Messiah of Jewish expectation and the Christ of Christian worship. Clearly this narrative is concerned with Christology in a very special way. We must add to this observation the fact that verse 8:29 marks a very definite stage of development in the Marcan presentation of the disciples' understanding of Jesus.[9] In the first half of the Gospel (1:16–8:21) the disciples are imperceptive in the sense that they appear incapable of perceiving who Jesus is. "Despite the continuous manifestation of Jesus' messiahship before the disciples in countless healings, exorcisms, and nature miracles, they remain amazingly obtuse in the face of their involvement in the messianic drama" (Weeden). The fact is that a careful perusal of the first half of Mark's Gospel creates the impression that the disciples, although granted special privileges in their relationship with Jesus, are far less perceptive concerning him than are other people who meet him in the course of his ministry.[10] With the Caesarea Philippi narrative, however, all this changes. True, the disciples are as dim-witted about Jesus as they had always been—note, for example, that Peter is presented as one who cannot accept the idea of a suffering Messiah even when that suffering culminates in resurrection (8:31 f.)—but now there is a change from imperceptivity to misconception. Whereas before they had not

[9]In this and what follows, we are indebted to some as yet unpublished work by Theodore J. Weeden of Wake Forest University on "The Heresy That Necessitated Mark's Gospel."

[10]Weeden, whom we are following at this point, refers to 5:28–31 where the disciples are oblivious to the healing power of Jesus' garments which was known to the hemorrhaging woman, to 8:4 where they have apparently gained no insight from the first feeding (6:30 ff.), and to 8:14–21 where they have failed to comprehend the supernatural capacity exhibited in the two feedings (6:30–44; 8:1–10).

been able to recognize Jesus as the Messiah, now they recognize him as Messiah but misunderstand the nature of that messiahship. Even this, however, is not the end. From Mark 14:10 onwards there is a further change in the disciples' understanding of Jesus. From this point on, they no longer simply misunderstand Jesus; now they totally reject him:[11] Judas betrays him; the inner group, Peter, James, and John, fails him in Gethsemane; Peter, the disciple par excellence, denies him adamantly in the High Priest's courtyard.

This presentation of the disciples' relationship to, and understanding of, Jesus bears all the hallmarks of a careful schematization and this fact focuses attention upon the Caesarea Philippi narrative as a part of a Marcan christological argument. There is every reason to believe that one of the problems faced by the early church was that of understanding the true nature of her Christology. In the Greek world it was natural to think of "divine men"—"sons of God," who by their miraculous powers demonstrated the divine reality that was present in them as substance or power and that enabled them to enjoy ecstatic appearances and to do miracles[12]—and therefore to think of Jesus in these terms. Not the least of the purposes of Mark's Gospel seems to have been specifically to combat a "divine man" understanding of Christology. In the first part of his Gospel, Mark goes to considerable pains to present Jesus in such a light; he saturates the first half of his Gospel with wonder-working activities of Jesus and intersperses summaries of this activity which can only be read in these terms (1:32 ff.; 3:7 ff.; 6:53 ff.) so that the reader of his Gospel is left with only one possible conclusion: Peter confesses Jesus as a "divine man." In fact, if 1:1–8:29 were the only extant section of the Gospel, one would be forced to believe that from the Marcan perspective the only authentic understanding of Jesus was as a "divine man-Messiah."

[11]The recognition of this fact is Weeden's special contribution to the discussion. Up to here he had been following, A. Kuby, "Zur Konzeption des Markus-Evangeliums," *Zeitschrift für die neutestamentliche Wissenschaft*, 49 (1958), 52–64, but the insights we follow from here on are his.
[12]Cf. R. H. Fuller, *The Foundations of New Testament Christology*, p. 98.

But it is precisely here that the Caesarea Philippi narrative plays its part. Here Peter confesses Jesus as the Messiah and goes on to interpret this messiahship in terms of a "divine man" Christology. Here, therefore, the Lord rejects this understanding of Christology in the most explicit terms possible: "Get behind me Satan! For you are not on the side of God, but of men" (8:33). The conclusion is inevitable: Mark presents a false understanding of Christology on the lips of Peter, a true understanding on the lips of Jesus. But in recognizing this, we are recognizing that the narrative is not concerned with the historical Peter's misunderstanding of the nature of Jesus' messiahship but with a false understanding of Christology prevalent in the church for which Mark is writing, i.e., with "the heresy that necessitated Mark's gospel" (Weeden). The purpose of the schematization of the disciples' misunderstanding of Jesus in Mark's Gospel is to press for an acceptance of a suffering servant Christology in the church for which Mark is writing.

One last aspect of this narrative which must concern us is that of the Messianic Secret (8:30).[13] At several places in our work we have had occasion to call attention to this feature of Mark's Gospel because the recognition of it as a feature of the Gospel rather than of the historical ministry of Jesus has been a key factor in the development of redaction criticism. At this point we have no need to repeat what we said earlier in the context of our discussions of Wrede and Lightfoot;[14] we shall simply add that anyone who would understand the theology of Mark has to wrestle with the meaning of the Messianic Secret in Mark. To review the various attempts to do this among contemporary scholars, or to make such an attempt ourselves, would be to go beyond the bounds of our present work; here we content ourselves with saying that this is one of the things redaction criticism has taught us to do.

We have concluded our discussion of the Caesarea Philippi

[13]See above, pp. 7 ff.
[14]See above, pp. 7–12 (Wrede), 23 f. (Lightfoot).

56

narrative in Mark and we now turn to a discussion of the parallels in Matthew and Luke: Matthew 16:13–28 and Luke 9:18–27. As we do, the situation changes because now we have the source which both Matthew and Luke have used. On literary-critical grounds[15] we can show that both Matthew and Luke have used Mark as a source for their own Gospels, and they are certainly following Mark in their account of this particular incident. This means that we can now move with certainty in regard to redaction criticism because a simple comparison of Matthew and Luke with Mark will immediately throw into relief the redactional activity of Matthew and Luke respectively. Whereas with Mark we have to spend a lot of time and energy attempting to reconstruct the tradition he has used if we are to detect his redactional activity on that tradition, with Matthew and Luke, in a narrative such as this one, we have the tradition they have used before us in the form in which it came to them from Mark. Our knowledge of the redactional activity of Matthew and Luke is therefore both firm and extensive; we not only have one of their major sources, Mark, but we can also reconstruct another, the sayings source, Q. It is no accident that redaction criticism is able to do spectacularly successful work on the theology of Matthew and the theology of Luke.

THE MATTHEAN NARRATIVE: MATTHEW 16:13–28

If we repeat our previous practice with Mark and begin by reading this narrative straight through, we notice at once that there is here not one incident but two. Matthew 16:13–23 is a story complete in itself which should be given some such heading as "The Revelation to Peter." Peter's confession is now greeted by the paean of praise: "Blessed are you, Simon Bar-Jona! For flesh and blood has not revealed this to you, but my Father who is in heaven," which throws it into stark relief both as a confession and as an insight made possible only by divine revelation. This "Revelation to Peter" is followed by the commissioning of Peter as formal head of the

---

[15]See the forthcoming volume in this series, W. A. Beardslee, *Literary Criticism of the New Testament*, and Perrin, *Rediscovering*, pp. 34 f.

church: "And I tell you, you are Peter, and on this rock I will build my church, and the powers of death shall not prevail against it. I will give you the keys of the kingdom of heaven, and whatever you bind on earth shall be bound in heaven, and whatever you loose on earth shall be loosed in heaven." This commissioning is clearly possible now because of the previous revelation; as the recipient of this revelation Peter fittingly becomes head of the Christian community. Then, in verse 21, there is a break in the narrative ("From that time Jesus began to show his disciples . . ."), and we get the transition to a second story, "The Misunderstanding of the Passion," an incident in which Matthew follows Mark in general content but with verbal changes that will concern us later.

The Matthean version is, then, a complete reworking of the narrative. Instead of a confession at Caesarea Philippi, we have both a revelation and a commissioning there, and the close connection between the confession and the subsequent misunderstanding characteristic of Mark, whose concerns are christological, is deliberately broken by Matthew, whose concerns are predominantly ecclesiological. This reworking is in part effected by verbal changes Matthew makes in the Marcan source, for example, Matthew's "From that time Jesus began" for Mark's "And he began" (Matt. 16:21; Mark 8:31), but for the most part they are due to the insertion of Matthew 16:17-19, a piece of tradition which has no parallel in Mark or Luke. Whence comes this formal blessing of Peter, this ceremonial appointment of him to hegemony in the early Christian church? The most probable answer (argued very strongly by R. H. Fuller in a paper "The 'Tu Es Petrus' Pericope" read to the Society of Biblical Literature on December 29, 1966) is that it is from a story which originally concerned Christ's resurrection appearance to Peter, a story used by Matthew here and which has also left its traces on other parts of the New Testament, but which is otherwise lost to us. The effect of the use of this piece of tradition by Matthew is unmistakable; it transforms the first part of the Marcan narrative into a new, self-contained incident in which

Peter is granted a heavenly revelation of Jesus' true nature as Messiah and in which, on the basis of this revelation, he assumes full authority as founder and leader of the early church with the power to determine not only membership of that church but also of the ultimate kingdom of God. Here we have not only "outside the church there is no salvation" but also "within the church salvation is certain."

At this point it is interesting to note that there is a certain conflict between Matthew himself and the tradition he is using. It is true enough that Matthew has a marked ecclesiological interest; every "Introduction to the New Testament" points out that the Gospel of Matthew is a "church book," designed to meet the ecclesiastical needs of a Christian congregation toward the end of the first century, and in this sense the changes in the first part of the Marcan narrative are absolutely typical of Matthew's total procedure. Matthew himself certainly believes that "outside the church there is no salvation," but he also believes that there are many in the church who are by no means saved and that good and bad will continue side by side in the church until the sorting out process of the final judgment.[16] In the tradition used by him in verses 17–19 of this narrative, however, there is no hint of any reservation in this matter; as we have already said, "within the church salvation is certain" is the viewpoint here! Very likely this tradition was the product of circles concerned with honoring Peter as founder and leader of the church as against possible rivals, and, as one might expect, a partisan viewpoint is accompanied by a somewhat unsophisticated view of the church. Be that as it may, Matthew uses the tradition here because he too honors Peter and because he is concerned with the moment of revelation as a consequence of which the church is founded.

It should be noted in passing that, if the supposition is correct that the tradition originally concerned a resurrection appearance to Peter, then we have here another most important insight into the nature of Gospel narratives as conceived

[16]Matt. 13:26–30; 13:47–50. Cf. G. Bornkamm, G. Barth, H. J. Held, *Tradition and Interpretation in Matthew*, pp. 19 ff.

by the evangelists themselves. Not only is Matthew following Mark in moving readily between the ministry of Jesus, which is past, and the ministry of the church, which is present, but he is also adding a third element in that he moves equally readily from the more distant past of the ministry of Jesus to the more immediate past of a resurrection appearance to Peter, to the present of the church. It is clear that in Gospel narratives past—both more distant and more immediate—and present flow into one another in a way that we must regard as remarkable.

If we consider the wording of that part of Matthew 16: 13–23 in which Matthew is following Mark, then two changes become immediately apparent: Jesus' first question, "Who do men say that I am," has become in Matthew, "Who do men say that the Son of man is," and Peter's confession, "You are the Christ," has become, "You are the Christ, the Son of the living God" (Matt. 16:13, 14). Both of these are significant. The first is part of a double change in that Matthew not only adds "Son of man" here but also rewrites the passion prediction (16:21, compare Mark 8:31) in order to avoid such a reference there; in effect he moves the "Son of man" reference from 16:21 to 16:13. Now the immediate effect of this is to make the question in 16:13 a nonsensical question, for the answer is now given in the question! It might be possible to suggest, as some commentators do, that "Son of man" here is a colorless self-designation, but this cannot be so because the fact that Matthew has moved the reference shows that it is for him a most meaningful one, and in any case in so heavily confessional a context as this the term must be regarded as being used confessionally. No, the truth of the matter is that Matthew is not here interested in a realistic question which will initiate a christological discussion, as is Mark; he is interested in the formal proclamation by Jesus of the existence of the Christian church and so "the sovereignty of the one who announces the period of his Church is solemnly enunciated at the beginning of the section" by using

60

the name "Son of man" "as an emphatic heading."[17] So he moves the term to the beginning of the section in order to make the Jesus who is to proclaim the existence and authority of the church, with Peter as its leader, also proclaim himself as Son of man. We shall have occasion to note below that for Matthew "Son of man" is a term of supreme authority. The second change, the addition of "the Son of the living God" to the confession, is simpler. Recognizing the confession for what it is, the regular confession of the early Christian church, Matthew has cast it in the form used in the circles in which he moved. "Son of God" was not a messianic title in pre-Christian Judaism and so the confession would be impossible in the historical circumstances of the ministry of Jesus—not that that is of any concern to Matthew. The confession developed in early Christianity and it is particularly meaningful to Matthew himself, no doubt having been mediated to him by the church for which he wrote. He has a strong interest in this particular christological title and in theological and devotional thinking based upon its use: Matthew 2:15; 8:29; 14:33; 11:25–27.

The second of the two incidents into which Matthew divides the Marcan Caesarea Philippi narrative is much closer to the original than is the first. The major change comes at the end where the climactic warning and promise in Mark have been reworked in the interest of a particular Matthean doctrine of the Son of man (Matt. 16:27, 28; cf. Mark 8:38; 9:1). The Marcan reference to the coming of the Son of man has been made much more emphatic: "For the Son of man is to come . . ."; and in place of the Son of man being "ashamed" we have a developed doctrine of the judgment of the Son of man: "and then he will repay every man for what he has done." This last is a development in the direction of Jewish apocalyptic (cf. I Enoch 45:3 and chapter 46), and it is a doctrine in which Matthew has a particular interest (Matt. 13:41; 25:31). More than this, the final "kingdom" of Chris-

[17]Tödt, *Son of Man*, p. 150. Tödt's discussion of the use of Son of man by Matthew here and elsewhere is most illuminating.

tian expectation can be for Matthew specifically the kingdom of the Son of man (see Matt. 13:41) and so the "before they see the kingdom of God come with power" of Mark 9:1 becomes, in Matthew 16:28, "before they see the Son of man coming in his kingdom." For Matthew "Son of man" is a title of supreme authority and that "Son of man" readily comes to assume functions which elsewhere in the Christian traditions are ascribed to God himself. Incidentally, the "Son of man" figure similarly assumes functions more normally attributed directly to God also in the Jewish apocalyptic traditions now represented by the so-called Similitudes of Enoch (I Enoch 37–71), traditions apparently known to Matthew.

THE LUCAN NARRATIVE: LUKE 9:18–27

This narrative begins with a verse that has long been the subject of discussion: "Now it happened that as he was praying alone the disciples were with him." This is nonsense, both in the English translation and in the original Greek, and the best explanation seems to be that Luke is deliberately combining the situation of Mark 6:46, "And after he had taken leave of them, he went into the hills to pray," with that of Mark 8:27, "And Jesus went on with his disciples...." When we add to this the oft-noted fact that Luke has no parallels to Mark 6:44–8:26, then it seems most probable that his copy of Mark's Gospel was defective at this point. Newly discovered papyrus codices of the Gospels offer us exact parallels to this: John 6:11–35 is missing from the codex designated P[66] and Luke 18:18–22:4 from that designated P[75].

As regards more theologically motivated redaction, there are two major changes in the Lucan pericope as over against the Marcan. The first of these is the omission of the dispute between Jesus and Peter (Mark 8:32 f.). We argued above that this was part of a literary device by means of which Mark makes an essential christological point. Luke is not interested in the christological point (note in Luke 22:24–30 his spectacular choice of a version of the dispute about greatness which enables him to omit Mark 10:45), and he therefore omits this part of the narrative. It may even be that he found it offensive, although this we cannot know.[18]

The second change is that by a series of subtle touches—for example, the insertion of "daily" in verse 23, and the omission of "in this adulterous and sinful generation" in verse 26 and of "come with power" in verse 27—Luke has completely changed the tenor of the whole passage. The Marcan note of urgency in the face of a specific persecution preceding an imminent eschaton has become a challenge for a continual witnessing over an indefinite period of time. This is part of the Lucan rethinking of early Christian eschatology to which Hans Conzelmann has so convincingly called our attention, and since his work is so readily available we need do no more than mention this fact here.

[18]If we are to think in these terms, then we could say that Matthew will have been able to maintain it because it is mitigated by the preceding approval of Peter in the Matthean version of the narrative. It is interesting to note that all three evangelists have the account of the Denial by Peter in their passion narratives (Mark 14:66–72; Matt. 26:69–75; Luke 22:56–61). The passion narrative in its essentials is certainly pre-Marcan and it may well have been this incident which led Mark to the literary device of the Petrine christological misunderstanding.

IV

The Significance of the Discipline

So far in this book we have attempted to describe the origins and characteristics of redaction criticism, to give some account of its first flowering, and to offer a sample of the kind of work which it attempts to do. We could go on to review the redaction-critical work that has been done since the accomplishments of Bornkamm and his pupils and of Marxsen and Conzelmann. But this work is still going on very actively indeed, and any summary attempted now would have to be drastically revised in light of the work that will no doubt be published within the next few years. It will be a decade or so at the very least before the work will have progressed far enough for there to be sufficient agreement among the scholars concerned to provide the basis for a summary of achieved results. All we could do today, for example, would be to show how Conzelmann's conclusions about the Lucan theology are in part accepted, in part modified, and in part rejected by those scholars who have responded to the challenge of his initial work on Luke-Acts. But the work is still going on and any such statement made now in the fall of 1969 would certainly have to be modified in the fall of 1970 because no doubt significant articles or even books on Luke using the redaction-critical methodology will appear in the next twelve months. The fact of the matter is that the work is being carried on so actively and the discipline and methodology are still so new that any attempt to present a summary of achievements or conclusions would be premature. So rather than attempt this in the final chapter of our book, we propose instead to reflect somewhat on what may turn out to be ultimately the significance of the discipline. In part this is to doff the mantle of a reporter and to put on that of a prophet, a wholly ridiculous proceeding, but some assessment of the possibilities inherent in the discipline and of its significance for broader theological concerns is essential in a book of this nature. For this reason the present writer will attempt some assessment of prospect and significance.

REDACTION AND COMPOSITION

It is becoming evident that one problem connected with redaction criticism is and will increasingly become the problem of the relationship between redaction and composition. This has come out at several points in our previous discussion, and we have called attention, for example, to the fact that Haenchen suggests the term "composition criticism" for the discipline. The problem is that in some respects we learn to recognize the theological motivation of a writer in the way he modifies or redacts previously existing material. It is for this reason, for example, that the term "redaction criticism" quite properly applies to the work of Conzelmann, who builds his basic understanding of the Lucan theology upon the minute observation of changes introduced by Luke in the material he inherits from Mark and Q; in other words, Conzelmann is looking for demonstrable tendencies to be revealed in Luke's handling of traditional material. Clearly wherever we have sources and the use of these as observable phenomena in the work of a writer, this is a proper methodology. This methodology can also be used in those cases where sources have to be posited rather than demonstrated as actually existing, for example, in the case of Mark. Here the present writer in a recent article has sought to define the traditional uses of Son of man inherited by Mark and then to observe the changes that he introduces in his use of this traditional material.[1] This again is redaction criticism. But we do not go very far in this direc-

[1]N. Perrin, "The Creative Use of the Son of Man Traditions by Mark," *Union Seminary Quarterly Review,* 23 (1967/68), 357–65.

tion before we come to the questions not only of the changes introduced in the material, but also the arrangement of the material, the movement of narrative in which the material is now set, and the like. This is composition, but it is also a good indicator of the theological purpose of the author. To give an obvious example, we learn a great deal about the Marcan theological purpose from the careful way in which he has composed a whole section of his Gospel, 8:27–10:52, to serve as an introduction to, and an exploration of, the meaning of the passion. And we gain further insight from the way in which he has developed within that section the careful threefold repetition of the pattern: passion prediction–misunderstanding–instruction in Christian discipleship.

Just as it is clear that we cannot easily separate redaction from composition, so it is also clear that we must expand the concept of composition to include the composition of wholly new sayings. Undoubtedly, many sayings now ascribed to Jesus in the synoptic Gospels were composed at various stages in the transmission of the tradition: Son of man sayings were composed by early Christian prophets, for example, or Mark 9:1 was composed by Mark to serve his own purpose as the climax to the Caesarea Philippi pericope. This kind of composition also speaks volumes for the theological purpose of the author. Here we have, therefore, a whole variety of activities in which an author engages, and the one thing that can be said of it all is that no single term is adequate to describe this variety. It is for this reason that we have stayed with the term "redaction criticism" rather than follow Haenchen's suggestion; "redaction criticism" may not be accurate but then no other term would be more so, and it does have the advantage of having been the first used in this context. But we wish to make it quite clear that we do understand "redaction criticism" as being a cipher rather than a description: it refers to the whole range of creative activities which we can detect in an evangelist, an author, a transmitter of tradition, and in which and by means of which we learn something of that author's, evangelist's, transmitter's theology. It may well be that one day the discipline will have developed to the point where composition criticism has to be distinguished from redaction criticism as redaction criticism now has to be distinguished from form criticism, but that day is not yet and we are concerned with the discipline as it is currently being practiced.

THE THEOLOGICAL HISTORY OF EARLIEST CHRISTIANITY

What can be said to be the significance of the discipline? First and most obvious is the fact that redaction criticism is vastly increasing our knowledge of the theological history of earliest Christianity. We have had occasion to stress that, while there are no agreed results as yet which could serve as the basis for summary presentations of, for example, the theology of Luke or the theology of Mark, there can be no doubt that the insights being gained through redaction criticism are of such importance that all previous presentations of the theology of the evangelists are now simply outdated. There can be no discussion of the theology of Luke which does not begin with the work of Conzelmann and go on from there, using his characteristic methodology; nor is it possible today to discuss any aspect of the theology of earliest Christianity without first considering what redaction criticism has had to say about it. We cannot possibly overstress the significance of the discipline in this field; there is no going back from it and there is no disputing it except on the basis of a better use of the characteristic methodology. So we may confidently expect that in the course of the next few years we are going to develop major understandings of the theology of the synoptic evangelists in a way that we could never have hoped to do before the rise of this discipline. Further, there can also be no doubt that we are going to be able to pinpoint other significant moments in the theological history of earliest Christianity. Already we have fundamentally important insights into the theology which produced the source Q, as has been demonstrated by the work of Tödt, and there is no reason why such knowledge should be limited to Q. At any point where we can isolate a moment in the development of tradition we are going to be able to say something about the theology which is at work in that moment and hence to fill in our knowledge of the theological history of earliest Christianity in a way that would have been impossible a few years ago. It must be said that the first chapters of all the standard histories of Christian doctrine or Christian theology are already out of date! Nor is it only the histories of Christian theology which are being affected by the development; the standard portrayals of New Testament theology, even Bultmann's, which is by far the most important of them all, are equally out of date insofar as they do not present the synoptic evangelists as major theologians. In this respect the theological world is going to be very seriously affected by the work of the redaction critic and, it is hoped, very considerably helped!

LIFE OF JESUS RESEARCH AND LIFE OF JESUS THEOLOGY

In addition to this quite obvious point there are some other things that must be said about the potential significance of redaction criticism, not the least of which is its significance in the context of Life of Jesus research and Life of Jesus theology. These are terms used by the Germans [*Leben Jesu Forschung, Leben Jesu Theologie*] to denote a particular attitude to the historical Jesus, namely, that of recognizing him as the locus of revelation and the central concern of Christian faith. Motivated by this viewpoint, whole generations of German scholars took up the "quest of the historical Jesus." In Germany this movement came to an end roughly with the rise of form criticism. In Britain and America, however, it has continued down to the present, and there is a constant tendency among us to regard the historical Jesus as all-important to faith and hence to want to continue to regard the Gospels as sources for knowledge of him. The present writer would be the first to admit that this is the motivation for the work that he did which led to his two previous books on *The Kingdom of God in the Teaching of Jesus* and *Rediscovering the Teaching of Jesus*. However, he must also be the first to admit that a growing awareness of the consequences of accepting form criticism, not only as a methodology to be used in Life of Jesus research but also as a way of understanding the nature of the Gospel narratives, has had grave consequences so far as this viewpoint is concerned. But it is when we come to redaction criticism that the whole matter comes to a head. For redaction criticism not only makes Life of Jesus research very much more difficult, it also raises fundamental questions with regard to the validity of a Life of Jesus theology. We will discuss each of these in turn.

That redaction criticism makes Life of Jesus research very much more difficult is, of course, immediately obvious. With the recognition that so very much of the material in the Gospels must be ascribed to the theological motivation of the evangelist or of an editor of the tradition, or of a prophet or preacher in the early church, we must come to recognize that the words of R. H. Lightfoot were fully and absolutely justified: the Gospels do indeed yield us "only the whisper of Jesus' voice." This means in practice that we must take as our starting point the assumption that the Gospels offer us directly information about the theology of the early church and not about the teaching of the historical Jesus, and that any information we may derive from them about Jesus can only come as a result of the stringent application of very carefully contrived criteria for authenticity. The present writer does not wish to belabor this point—he has made it already in the first chapter of his *Rediscovering the Teaching of Jesus*—but it must be said once again here since this is the first and most immediate impact of redaction criticism upon one who has grown up in Anglo-Saxon theological circumstances. What has happened in practice is that over the last fifty years or so we have seen the gradual recognition that very stringent criteria indeed are necessary in the quest for authentic words of Jesus. There was a time when anything that was not obviously impossible on the lips of Jesus was ascribed to him. Again at a more sophisticated level we saw the day when there was a tendency to feel that the Gospel tradition was only one step removed from actual reminiscence of the ministry of Jesus and so any convergence of two sources in the synoptic tradition brought us into that ministry. This was essentially the position of the present writer's first teacher, T. W. Manson. In all of this there was the unspoken assumption that the burden of proof lay on the claim to inauthenticity. This attitude is still to be detected in some work, especially that coming from England. An example would be the recent book *The Son of Man in Mark* by Morna D. Hooker.[2] Miss Hooker is convinced that form criticism has failed to make its point, and she is therefore content with the assumption that may be caricatured in the words, "If it could have come from Jesus it most probably did." But it is the contention of our present book that neither form criticism nor redaction criticism has failed; rather they have succeeded spectacularly in illuminating the true nature of the Gospel tradition; hence the burden of proof must lay on the claim to authenticity, and the difficulties of establishing that claim become very great—very great indeed, but not impossible. The present writer would be the first to claim that we do know something about Jesus and that it is possible to establish some conclusions with regard to his teaching But it is by no means simple, and the sooner this is recognized, the better for Life of Jesus research.

The actual needs of the situation here can perhaps best be illustrated by reference to the specific methodologies proposed for Life of Jesus research by R. H. Fuller and the present writer.[3] Both of us worked in full knowledge of the impact of form criticism (a term used so as to include what we are here calling redaction criticism); we both had the same concern—to find a way to recognize authentic Jesus material in the synoptic tradition—and we worked completely independently of one another. The measure of agreement we reached is therefore all the more striking.

We agree that what is needed first and foremost is a history of the tradition. We must follow in the path of R. Bultmann in his *History of the Synoptic Tradition* or J. Jeremias in his *Parables of Jesus* and reconstruct the history of the particular tradition with which we are concerned, i.e., the history of its transmission in the church, so that we may reach its primary stratum. When we have reached that form of the material

[2]London: SPCK, 1967. See the present writer's review of this book in the *Journal of the American Academy of Religion*, 37(1969), 92–94.
[3]R. H. Fuller, *A Critical Introduction to the New Testament* (Naperville: Allenson, 1966), pp. 91–104; N. Perrin, *Rediscovering*, pp. 15–49.

we must then devise criteria by means of which we can test its authenticity. Both Fuller and the present writer devised the same three criteria although we gave them different names.

First and most important, we have the criterion of "distinctiveness" (Fuller) or "dissimilarity" (Perrin): material may be ascribed to Jesus only if it can be shown to be distinctive of him, which usually will mean dissimilar to known tendencies in Judaism before him or the church after him. An example of this would be the address to God, "Abba" (Father), in the Lucan version of the Lord's Prayer. Jeremias has shown that this is foreign to the Judaism of Jesus' day, and the Matthean version of the Lord's Prayer, representing the more characteristic piety of the early church, moves away from it. Then we have, secondly, the "cross-section method" (Fuller) or "criterion of multiple attestation" (Perrin): material may be accepted which is found in a multiplicity of sources or forms of tradition, provided always that this multiple attestation is not due to the influence of some widespread church practice such as the Eucharist. An example here would be the concern of Jesus for "tax collectors and sinners." Thirdly and lastly, we have the criterion of "consistency" (Fuller) or "coherence" (Perrin): material which is consistent with or coheres with material established as authentic by other means may also be accepted. It is to be acknowledged, of course, that in all this the material must also pass linguistic and environmental tests. Anything which is clearly Greek in origin, such as the explanation of the Sower in Mark 4:11-20, or which obviously reflects the environment of the church, such as the commissioning of Peter in Matthew 16:18 f., must be rejected. At the same time material which is both Aramaic and Palestinian must also meet other criteria, since the Aramaic-speaking Palestinian church certainly created Jesus material, as for example, apocalyptic Son of man sayings.

From this moment forward Life of Jesus research must proceed in this way and use this kind of methodology. The impact of form and redaction criticism is such that nothing less than this kind of stringency is possible. It is quite clear that form criticism and its "lusty infant," redaction criticism, have made Life of Jesus research immensely more difficult than it was at one time held to be, and that, at the same time, scholarship is moving ahead in the attempt to meet the challenge of these difficulties. But the fact that redaction criticism makes Life of Jesus research immensely more difficult is not the real cutting edge of its impact in this field, even if it is the most obvious thing about it. The real cutting edge of the impact of redaction criticism is the fact that it raises very serious questions indeed about that which normally motivates Life of Jesus research: Life of Jesus theology. It raises above all the question as to whether the view of the historical Jesus as the locus of revelation and the central concern of Christian faith is in fact justifiable, and it raises this question because it shows how truly foreign such a view is to the New Testament itself.

It has, of course, always been clear that the very conception of the "historical Jesus" was foreign to the New Testament as such a conception would be to any document from the ancient world. When we use the word "historical" we mean "factual," "as it actually was," or the like, and our intention is always to distinguish between this and later additions or interpretations. But the ancient world simply did not think in this way, and so we always have the problem of recovering the historical figure, as we would understand that phrase, from documents which do not observe our distinctions. In this respect the problem is the same whether the figure be Jesus, Julius Caesar, or Socrates; we have to set out on a "quest" of the historical figure. Further, and equally obviously, we have to contend with the fact that the ancient documents were written by people with a view of the world very different from our own. To the men of the New Testament, for example, the appearance of angels, the machinations of demons, the breaking open of the heavens to facilitate the descent of a dove or the ascent of a body are all events within the realm of realistic expectation, whereas the appearance of such things to us would send us to consult either an oculist or a psychiatrist! But none of this is new, and certainly none of it is due to the impact of redaction criticism. It was always well-known to scholars who engaged in the "quest of the historical Jesus"[4] and they developed techniques for dealing with the problems involved. The fact that the Gospels are not historical sources in our sense of that phrase does not mean that historical information cannot be derived from them. In this regard the difference made by the insights of redaction criticism is simply that the "quest" becomes more difficult, but, as we have already indicated, historical scholarship is rising to meet that particular challenge.

The really complicating factor in the case of the New Testament documents, more specifically the Gospels, is that the early church, not having our sense of the word "historical" and being motivated by an intense religious experience, saw no reason to distinguish between words originally spoken by the historical Jesus bar Joseph from Nazareth and words ascribed to him in the tradition of the church. In this respect the New Testament is very different from the records we have of Jewish rabbis or Greek teachers in the ancient world. In every instance, whether it be the Greek philosopher Socrates, the Jewish rabbi Johanan ben Zakkai, or Jesus of Nazareth, we would have the problem of distinguishing the original core of authentic material from accretions or interpretations in the particular tradition concerned, but in the case of the New Testament there is something else to consider: the sense of the presence of the risen Lord Jesus in the experience of the believer or the church and the conviction that this Jesus who speaks *is* the Jesus who once spoke. It is at this point that redaction criticism makes its impact, for it reveals to us how very much of the material ascribed to the Jesus who spoke in Galilee or Judea must in fact be ascribed to the Jesus who spoke through a prophet or evangelist in the early church. We saw in our discussion of the Caesarea Philippi pericope, for example, that in the case of the two climactic sayings ascribed to Jesus in Mark 8:38 and 9:1, the first is ultimately from a Christian prophet and the second is a composition of the evangelist himself. Further, we saw that in the Matthean version of that pericope the key commissioning of Peter, Matthew

*The allusion is to the title of Albert Schweitzer's famous book.

73

16:18 f., was very likely originally known to Matthew himself as a commissioning by the risen Lord in a resurrection story but is then ascribed by him to the Jesus of the Gospel story. But that is precisely the point: "the Jesus of the Gospel story" is at one and the same time the "historical" Jesus bar Joseph from Nazareth, the risen Lord of Peter's resurrection vision, and the Son of God who guides the evangelist to an understanding of the ultimate hope for persecuted Christians.

It is this aspect of the Gospel narratives which redaction criticism so clearly reveals. It makes clear the fact that the voice of the Jesus of the Gospels is the voice of living Christian experience, and that the evangelists and the tradition they represent are indifferent as to whether this experience is ultimately related to anything said or done in Galilee or Judea before the crucifixion. In light of this fact it seems very hard indeed to justify a Life of Jesus theology. If the Jesus of the Gospel of Mark is the Jesus of Mark's own Christian experience and that of the church before him, then the claim that the "historical" Jesus is the center and source of Christian faith would seem to have no necessary basis in the New Testament. It has always been clear that neither Paul, John, nor the Catholic epistles have the kind of attitude toward the earthly Jesus that would justify a central place for the historical Jesus in Christian theology It is no accident that the rise of a Life of Jesus theology was closely connected with an acceptance of the Marcan hypothesis. In destroying the Marcan hypothesis redaction criticism would seem to have cut the ground from under the feet of that theology.

THE NATURE OF A "GOSPEL"

But this negative observation is by no means the end of the matter. Redaction criticism has done much more than make it difficult to justify a Life of Jesus theology: it has revealed something of the nature of a "Gospel." We must always remember that the form "Gospel" is the one unique literary product of New Testament Christianity. There are literary parallels to all the other kinds of literature represented in the New Testament. Other people produced letters, chronicles of the acts of famous men, apocalyptic discourses, but only the early Christians produced "Gospels." The literary form "Gospel" is the unique product of early Christianity and as such must be held to be characteristic of a distinctive element in early Christian faith. Not the least of the services of redaction criticism is that it is indicating to us something of the true nature of that form. In revealing the extent to which the theological viewpoint of the evangelist or transmitter of the tradition has played a part in the formation of the Gospel material, it is forcing us to recognize that a Gospel does not portray the history of the ministry of Jesus from A.D. 27–30, or whatever the dates may actually have been, but the history of Christian experience in any and every age. At the same time this history of Christian experience is cast in the form of a chronicle of the ministry of Jesus, and some parts of it— whether large or small is irrelevant at this point—are actually based on reminiscence of that ministry. The Gospel of Mark is the prototype which the others follow and it is a mixture of historical reminiscence, interpreted tradition, and the free creativity of prophets and the evangelist. It is, in other words, a strange mixture of history, legend, and myth. It is this fact which redaction criticism makes unmistakably clear; and it is this fact to which we have to do justice in our thinking about the significance of the "Gospel" as the characteristic and distinctive literary product of early Christianity.

We have already seen the negative impact of this in the difficulties it creates for Life of Jesus research and the doubts it casts upon the validity of a Life of Jesus theology. We now have to look at the other side of the coin and ask what positive impact it has upon us as we think about the essential nature of Christian faith. Here it would seem that there are two things immediately to be said. As revealed by redaction criticism the nature of a Gospel is such that it must be held that the locus of revelation is not the ministry of the historical Jesus but the reality of Christian experience; however, it is also clear that there is real continuity between those two things.

The Gospels as we have them, as well as the traditions that lie behind them, reflect the experience of early Christianity.

75

The teaching of Jesus was first collected, as the redaction-critical work on the Q material shows, in order to continue Jesus' eschatological proclamation. It was believed that the resurrection had vindicated Jesus and his proclamation of the kingdom of God and that therefore the future hope represented by that proclamation was still valid, indeed, more valid now than ever because of the act of God in vindicating Jesus. So the proclamation was continued, although the form of the hope changed from the general expectation of the eschatological activity of God, represented by the term "kingdom of God," to the concrete picture of that activity in the form of the coming of Jesus as Lord or Son of man. In the context of this hope the proclamation of Jesus was carried on as the proclamation of the early church, and the teaching of Jesus was carried on as preparation for his coming as Lord.

This is the moment at which the tradition represented by the Gospels begins, and it is at this moment that the nature of the continuity between Jesus and the early church can be seen. The resurrection vindicated Jesus as eschatological prophet and revealed him as Lord; the early church, convinced of this, proclaimed his coming as he had proclaimed the coming of the kingdom and prepared herself for that coming by reiterating his teaching as showing what men must do to stand well at that coming. So the continuity here is very real, and the historical Jesus must be held to be of significance to the faith of earliest Christianity. But Jesus is significant not primarily because of what he had done in the past in his earthly ministry but because of what he was to do at his future coming as Lord or Son of man. It is the hope of the future that gives significance to the memory of the past. Moreover, that hope was motivated not so much by the disciples' experience of the past ministry as by their experience of the present reality of Jesus as risen.

From the very beginning, therefore, we have essentially the situation which was to be characteristic of New Testament Christianity and which was to be reflected in the creation of the literary form "Gospel." It might be described as a situation in which distinctions between past, present, and future tended to be lost as the present experience of Jesus as risen led to a new understanding of the future and of the past. The key was the present experience without which the future would have appeared barren and the past would have been soon forgotten. But because of that experience there came the conviction that the Jesus who had been known would be known again.

So far as the formation of Gospel tradition is concerned, one way to arrive at an understanding of the matter might be to consider the formation of Son of man sayings. The eschatological hope of the early church is expressed by the creation of apocalyptic Son of man sayings such as that now found in Mark 8:38, which we have previously discussed. At the same time other sayings are created in which the future authority of Jesus as Son of man is expressed in terms of his past ministry, the clearest being Mark 2:10 ("that you may know that the Son of man has authority on earth to forgive sins") and 2:28 ("so the Son of man is lord even of the sabbath"). In these sayings Jesus is already acting with the authority with which he will act when he comes as Son of man. In other words the past ministry of Jesus is seen in light of the expectation of his future ministry as Son of man. Now we are at the heart of the matter, for we can see that past, present, and future have flowed together and in so doing have led to the formation of Gospel-type material. The future ministry of the Son of man and the past ministry of Jesus are one and the same. "Jesus Christ is the same, yesterday, today, and forever," so the expectation for the future can be expressed in the form of sayings or stories from the past. At the same time it must also have been true that the memory of the past ministry of Jesus gave form and content to the expectation of the future. But the important thing is the abandonment of any distinction between past and future, between future and past, revealed in the process of the formation of Son of man sayings, which in this respect are typical of Gospel-type tradition altogether.

The next step is to recognize the importance of the present experience which led to the prophetic utterance of apocalyptic Son of man sayings such as Mark 8:38. The very fact that such sayings were produced reveals the existence of a conviction that the Lord who spoke is the Lord who speaks. In taking up the Jesus material, the early church not only reinterpreted it to fit the needs of a new situation, but also, as redaction criticism has shown, she did much more. The point we would make here is that the church could treat the material with such freedom only because of a conviction that the Lord who spoke is the Lord who speaks. Without this conviction there would have been no Gospel material; when such a conviction is assumed a particular feature of Gospel material—the representation of the present in the form of an account of the past—becomes readily understandable.

We see, therefore, that Gospel material represents a flowing together of past, present, and future. It takes the form of stories and sayings from the past because the Jesus who speaks is the Jesus who spoke and because the Jesus to come as Lord/ Son of man is the Jesus who came as eschatological prophet. But both the view of the past which it represents and the hope for the future which it expresses are due to an experience in the present. There could have been no Gospel at all without the conviction that Jesus was to be known in the present as risen, and there would have been no Gospel of Mark without the conviction that the risen Lord had a message for the church for which Mark wrote. In respect to motivation the Gospels are not different from the letters to the seven churches in the Book of Revelation; they are a message from the risen Lord addressed to his church. But in respect to form they are very different indeed, and the reason for this difference is what distinguishes early Christianity from other apocalyptic sects in ancient Judaism: the conviction that the Lord of the future is the Jesus of his past earthly ministry and of the Christian's present experience of him as risen. For this reason the message to the present takes the form of stories and sayings from the past.

Perhaps the most important thing which redaction criticism has done for us to date is to confront us with this understanding of the essential nature of "Gospel" material. The Gospels are the characteristic and unique literary product of early

Christianity, and hence an understanding of their essential nature must be of significance to an understanding of the essential nature of the faith they represent. Redaction criticism is teaching us that the content of a Gospel is as much a product of the present experience of the men who transmitted the tradition and of the evangelist, as apocalyptic literature is a product of the seer's visions. John's letter to the church at Ephesus (Rev. 2:1) is a product of his experience on the island of Patmos "in the Spirit on the Lord's day" (Rev. 1:10). But whereas the apocalyptic seer expresses his experience in terms of the world of apocalyptic imagery, the evangelist expresses his in terms of the past ministry of Jesus and in so doing strikes the note that is characteristically Christian.

We can now return to the double point we made at the beginning of our discussion of this aspect of the significance of the impact of redaction criticism. As revealed by redaction criticism the nature of the Gospels and of Gospel material is such that the locus of revelation must be held to be in the present of Christian experience. At the same time that experience must be continuous with the past of the ministry of Jesus, knowledge of which will both condition and inform it.

Glossary

APOCALYPTIC From a Greek root meaning "to uncover," this word is used to describe the literature produced to reveal the secrets of the coming of the End Time. In the Old Testament the book of Daniel is an apocalyptic work, as is Revelation in the New Testament. The apocalyptic movement was very strong in both Judaism and Christianity into the second century A.D.

CHRISTOLOGY The doctrine of the person of Christ.

DOGMA, DOGMATIC From the Greek word for opinion, an opinion held or taught as true and more especially a theological opinion or doctrine so held or taught.

ESCHATOLOGY From the Greek word for "end" (*eschaton*), it refers to teaching concerning the end of time or history.

EVANGELIST The author of a Gospel, the Greek word for the Gospel being *euangelion* which was rendered into English as "evangel."

PAROUSIA From a Greek word meaning "presence," especially the presence of a king or high official visiting a given locality, this word was used by the evangelist Matthew of the "second coming" of Christ and so passed into the vocabulary of the church with the meaning, "the final coming (of Christ) in full authority and power."

Q The first letter of the German word *Quelle* (source); it is used to designate the source of the material which Matthew and Luke have in common which does not come from Mark. Since this material is almost wholly teaching ascribed to Jesus, the expression "sayings source" is sometimes also used.

80

SITZ IM LEBEN   The German phrase "setting in life" is used as a technical term by form critics to denote the aspect of early Christian practice (liturgy, exhortation, apologetic, catechetical instruction, etc.) in the context of which a given form of tradition functions.

SON OF MAN   One of the titles used by the early Christians of Jesus; like others of a similar nature (e.g., Son of God, Son of David) it has its roots in the Old Testament (Dan. 7) and it is used in the *apocalyptic* literature (I Enoch, IV Ezra). The use of this title in the New Testament presents many problems to the scholar; indeed, almost everything about it is disputed. A statement of what is probably the most widely held position today with regard to the matter will be found in the relevant sections of R. H. Fuller, *Foundations of New Testament Christology* (New York: Charles Scribner's Sons, 1965). A preliminary statement of the present writer's views, which differ at some important points, will be found in N. Perrin, *Rediscovering the Teaching of Jesus* (New York: Harper & Row, 1967), pp. 164–99.

SYNOPTIC GOSPELS   The Gospels of Matthew, Mark, and Luke, so called because they can be set side by side and read together, whereas the Gospel of John is very different in outline, content, and style. "Synoptic" is from a Greek root meaning "to view together."

TRADITION   From a Latin root meaning "to hand down," this word denotes material handed down or passed on in the church. In form and redaction criticism the concept of tradition plays an important part because it is recognized that much of the material now found in the New Testament texts was used in a variety of ways in the church before it was given its present form by the actual author of the particular New Testament text concerned. In other words, the material has a history in the tradition (of the church).

Annotated Bibliography

This bibliography is designed as a guide to students and is deliberately limited to works readily available; moreover, the material in languages other than English has been kept to a minimum.

THE WORKS OF R. H. LIGHTFOOT

LIGHTFOOT, R. H. *History and Interpretation in the Gospels.* ("The Bampton Lectures," 1934.) New York: Harper and Bros., no date. This, the pioneer work in the field, is discussed in chapter I above. Lightfoot followed it up with two further works, both of which are still important today.

――――. *Locality and Doctrine in the Gospels.* New York and London: Harper and Bros., no date. This is a series of studies in all four Gospels.

――――. *The Gospel Message of St. Mark.* ("Oxford Paperbacks.") Oxford (England): University Press, 1962. Six studies of Mark, one of John, and an apologetic for form criticism.

THE GOSPEL OF MATTHEW

BORNKAMM, G., BARTH, G., HELD, H. J. *Tradition and Interpretation in Matthew.* Translated by PERCY SCOTT. Philadelphia: Westminster Press, 1963. The fundamental work on Matthew, this book is discussed in chapter II above.

HARE, DOUGLAS R. A. *The Theme of Jewish Persecution of Christians in the Gospel According to St. Matthew.* ("Society for New Testament Studies, Monograph Series," No. 6.) Cambridge: University Press, 1967. A study of the historical background of Jewish-Christian relations in the first century, and a redaction-critical exegesis of Matthean passages relevant to this topic, followed by considerations of the theological perspective from which Matthew views the conflict between his community and Judaism.

KINGSBURY, J. D. *The Parables of Jesus in Matthew 13.* Richmond: John Knox Press, 1969. Kingsbury studies the parables in relation to Matthew's historical setting and theology. He argues that chapter 13 is a turning point in the gospel where Jesus turns from Israel to the disciples as the true people of God.

SUGGS, M. JACK. *Wisdom, Law and Christology in Matthew's Gospel.* Cambridge: Harvard University Press, 1970. A redaction-critical study of wisdom motifs as they appear in the Christologies of Q and Matthew.

THOMPSON, WILLIAM G. *Matthew's Advice to a Divided Community: Mt. 17,22–18,35.* ("Analecta Biblica," No. 44.) Rome: Biblical Institute Press, 1970. Thompson studies the composition of the above section of Matthew and finds behind the composition a concrete situation of a community experiencing persecution from without and tension from within in the form of mutual hatred, the rise of false prophets and widespread scandal.

THE GOSPEL OF MARK

MARXSEN, W. *Der Evangelist Markus. Studien zur Redaktionsgeschichte des Evangeliums.* Göttingen: Vandenhoeck & Ruprecht, ¹1956, ²1959. The basic work on Mark, this book is discussed in chapter II above. An English translation entitled *Mark the Evangelist* (New York and Nashville: Abingdon Press, 1969) has appeared.

ROBINSON, J. M. *The Problem of History in Mark.* ("Studies in Biblical Theology," No. 21.) Naperville: Allenson, 1957. This was actually written before Marxsen's work and is not explicitly an example of the redaction-critical method. But in its concern for a major aspect of the Marcan theology, it moves in the same general direction.

BURKILL, T. A. *Mysterious Revelation: An Examination of the Philosophy of St. Mark's Gospel.* Ithaca: Cornell University Press, 1963. A series of studies centering around the Messianic Secret motif in Mark. We saw in chapter I above how important this motif has proven to be in the development of redaction criticism as a discipline.

BEST, ERNEST. *The Temptation and the Passion: The Marcan Soteriology.* ("Society for New Testament Studies Monograph

Series," No. 2.) New York: Cambridge University Press, 1965. A strange book in that the author combines redaction criticism with the assumption "that Mark believes that the incidents he uses actually happened" (p. xi)!

KNIGGS, HANS DIETER. "The Meaning of Mark." *Interpretation* 22 (1968), pp. 53–70. Excellent survey of recent (mostly German) work on Messianic secret and theology of Mark.

PERRIN, NORMAN. "The Christology of Mark: A Study in Methodology." *Journal of Religion* 51 (July, 1971). An attempt to develop and define a methodology for the application or redaction criticism to the gospel of Mark, and to exhibit it in a study of the Christology of the gospel.

THE GOSPEL OF LUKE AND THE ACTS OF THE APOSTLES

CONZELMANN, H. *The Theology of St. Luke.* Translated by G. BUSWELL. New York: Harper and Row, 1960. This truly epoch-making book was discussed in chapter II above.

Of the many German responses to Conzelmann's work only one has been translated into English:

FLENDER, H. *St. Luke: Theologian of Redemptive History.* Translated by REGINALD H. and ILSA FULLER. Philadelphia: Fortress Press, 1967.

An American response to Conzelmann is:

BROWN, SCHUYLER. *Apostasy and Perseverance in the Theology of Luke.* ("Analecta Biblica," No. 36.) Rome: Biblical Institute Press, 1969. Brown criticizes Conzelmann's sharp distinction between the age of Jesus and the age of the church. Luke and Acts are united by a motif of the disciples' faithfulness in the face of *peirasmos* (temptation).

Others in German include:

BARTSCH, H. W. *Wachet aber zu jeder Zeit! Entworf einer Auslegung des Lukas-Evangeliums.* Hamburg-Bergstedt: H. Reich, 1963.

There is a volume of essays in English, many of which reflect the impact of Conzelmann:

Studies in Luke-Acts. Essays presented in Honor of Paul Schubert. Edited by LEANDER E. KECK and J. LOUIS MARTYN. Nashville and New York: Abingdon Press, 1966.

Specific studies of the Acts of the Apostles reflecting the concerns of redaction criticism include:

O'NEILL, J. C. *The Theology of Acts in its Historical Setting.* London: SPCK, 1961.

HAENCHEN, E. *Die Apostelgeschichte.* ("Meyer Kommentar.") Göttingen: Vandenhoeck & Ruprecht, 1956. One of the great commentaries, as epoch-making in its own way as Conzelmann's book.

CONZELMANN, H. *Die Apostelgeschichte.* ("Handbuch zum Neuen Testament.") Tübingen: J. C. B. Mohr (Paul Siebeck), 1963. Conzelmann completes his own work on Luke-Acts with a commentary on Acts.

THE GOSPEL OF JOHN

Redaction-critical work on John is in its infancy, but a start has been made.

MARTYN, J. LOUIS. *History and Theology in the Fourth Gospel.* New York: Harper & Row, 1968. The author distinguishes between tradition and redaction in the case of four blocks of Johannine material, all miracle stories, and then goes on to draw conclusions both about the theology of John and about the historical situation in the church in which John was writing.

FORTNA, ROBERT T. *The Gospel of Signs.* ("Society for New Testament Studies, Monograph Series," No. 11.) Cambridge: University Press, 1970. Fortna attempts to isolate a pre-Johannine narrative source, a signs source, and to study the Johannine reinterpretation of that source in the gospel proper.

REDACTION-CRITICAL APPROACHES TO THE CHRISTOLOGY OF THE NEW TESTAMENT

Redaction criticism has proven invaluable as a new method of approach to long-standing problems. The work available in English is mostly connected with the Christology of the New Testament.

TÖDT, H. E. *The Son of Man in the Synoptic Tradition.* Translated by DOROTHEA M. BARTON. Philadelphia: Westminster Press, 1965. Tödt's work is remarkable as a first attempt to use redaction criticism in approaching the extraordinarily difficult problems presented by the use of Son of man in the synoptic Gospels and in the traditions which lie behind them. On the whole a very successful piece of work, especially in its theology of Q.

HAHN, FERDINAND. *The Titles of Jesus in Christology.* New York and Cleveland: World Publishing Co., 1969. Hahn investigates the strands of tradition lying behind the use of the various christological titles in the Gospels, especially in the Gospel of Mark. Again, the force and value of redaction criticism comes through very strongly in this work.

FULLER, R. H. *The Foundations of New Testament Christology.* New York: Charles Scribner's Sons, 1965. A book which fully utilizes the insights developed by Tödt and Hahn. Written for a more general audience, it is a valuable introduction to new methods of studying the Christology of the New Testament.

PERRIN, NORMAN. "The Son of Man in the Synoptic Tradition." *Biblical Research* 13 (1968), pp. 1–23. A study of the origin and use of Son of Man with special emphasis on the Marcan redaction of Son of Man traditions and the importance of this to his Gospel.

PERRIN, NORMAN. "The Creative Use of the Son of Man Traditions by Mark." *Union Seminary Quarterly Review* 23 (1968), pp. 357–365. A fuller development of an aspect of the above article.

PERRIN, NORMAN. "The Christology of Mark." See under The Gospel of Mark.

GENERAL

MARXSEN, W. *Introduction to the New Testament.* Translated by G. BUSWELL. Philadelphia: Fortress Press, 1968. This is an introduction to the New Testament as a whole by a leading redaction critic. Unfortunately it does not include any discussion of the discipline as such but insights developed by its use are to be found in the discussion of the synoptic Gospels and Acts.

ROHDE, J. *Rediscovering the Teaching of the Evangelists.* Translated by D. M. BARTON. Philadelphia: Westminster Press, 1969. Originally an East German doctoral dissertation, this book is a survey of the origin and development of redaction criticism in Germany (non-German work is ignored). The author presents valuable summaries of all the pertinent books and articles. The book appeared too late to be used in the text of the present volume, but it would be a natural "next step" for the reader who wished to pursue the matter further.